The Field Guide

FOR SMALL GROUP LEADERS

Updated and
Expanded

The Field Guide

FOR SMALL GROUP LEADERS

Equipping Everyday Believers
for Life-Changing Community

SAM O'NEAL

THOMAS NELSON®
Since 1798

THOMAS NELSON

The Field Guide for Small Group Leaders
Copyright © 2012, 2023 by Write Great Stories, Inc.

Published in Nashville, Tennessee, by Thomas Nelson. Thomas Nelson is a registered trademark of HarperCollins Christian Publishing, Inc.

Thomas Nelson titles may be purchased in bulk for educational, business, fundraising, or sales promotional use. For information, please e-mail SpecialMarkets@ThomasNelson.com.

Library of Congress Cataloging-in-Publication Data

Names: O'Neal, Sam, 1981- author.
Title: The field guide for small group leaders : equipping everyday believers for life-changing community / Sam O'Neal.
Description: Nashville : Thomas Nelson, 2023.
Identifiers: LCCN 2022058150 (print) | LCCN 2022058151 (ebook) | ISBN 9780310144533 (softcover) | ISBN 9780310144670 (audiobook) | ISBN 9780310144540 (ebook)
Subjects: LCSH: Small groups—Religious aspects—Christianity. | Group ministry. | Church group work. | Christian leadership.
Classification: LCC BV652.2 .O542 2023 (print) | LCC BV652.2 (ebook) | DDC 253/.7—dc23/eng/20230302
LC record available at https://lccn.loc.gov/2022058150
LC ebook record available at https://lccn.loc.gov/2022058151

Cover design: Derek Thornton / Notch Design
Cover photos: © Canbedone / Shutterstock; Public Domain
Interior design: Denise Froehlich

Printed in the United States of America

23 24 25 26 27 28 29 30 31 32 33 /TRM/ 15 14 13 12 11 10 9 8 7 6 5 4 3 2 1

Contents

➐ Foreword

Fifteen years ago I started meeting weekly with a group of friends. Some were good friends. Some I didn't know too well. Some were confident in their relationship with God, and others had no idea what they believed. When it came to a "small group" or "doing life together," none of us knew what we were doing. Not really. That included me.

We just knew we were tired of the status quo. Tired of carrying the weight, shame, and consequences of our sin. Our shoulders weren't made for that. We were also tired of watching the enemy take ground in our families, communities, and churches.

Personally, I'd been reading Acts and comparing the lives of the apostles with mine—and one of these was not like the others.

If I could condense everything our group members wanted into a single word, it would be *freedom*. What would it look like to walk in the freedom Jesus promises? We really had no idea what that would look like, but we knew the enemy's stated goal is to steal, kill, and destroy, and we'd had enough of that.

So we circled up and started walking. Together. In and through God's Word. Then the Lord did a really cool thing. He knit us together in such a way that we grew to trust each other. A beautiful gift.

As I look in the rearview mirror at those fifteen years, I'm amazed at everything we've experienced. "Signs and wonders" come to mind. We have seen honest-to-goodness miracles, stuff I can't explain other than to say God is able and God is good. We've seen demons cast out, addictions healed, and generational curses broken for good. We've laughed, cried, prayed, and worshiped our faces off.

Most importantly, we've fallen more in love with Jesus. And each other.

I said all that to say this: I'm a fan of small groups. I believe in the life-changing power of community and intentional discipleship. If you're not in one, you should be. Lone Rangers make really bad disciples.

That's why I'm thankful you've found this book.

I've known Sam for years. We've worked together, broken bread together, and prayed for each other. He loves God's Word and has made it the foundation of this book—this field guide for group leaders. He understands discipleship and community and growth, but he also understands the nuts and bolts of creating an environment where those concepts can become reality.

One of the things I appreciate most about this *Field Guide for Small Group Leaders* is Sam's emphasis on life-change, on transformation. Biblical community was never intended to be centered on thinking and talking. What we know and learn should, through the power of the Holy Spirit, migrate down out of our heads and into our hearts where we walk it out. That's why Jesus said, "Follow me." When we do, we will look and sound different. Because we are.

Let me warn you on the front end that this stuff can be messy. Which is good. God does His best work in our messes.

If you don't have a group of friends, and you don't know where to start, then just pray: "Lord, I want to do life with other believers. Help." You might be surprised who He brings to the circle. When He does, I pray the Lord meets you in and through the words in this book, that you laugh, cry, pray, repent, forgive, and worship your faces off, and that you walk in freedom.

CHARLES MARTIN

 Preface

The happiest moment of my life took place during a small group gathering.

It was October 13, 2002. I had finished my undergraduate work a few months earlier and was living in a house with five of my best friends from school. I was also deeply in love with a beautiful young woman named Jessica, and on that crisp day in Wheaton, Illinois, I was about to ask for her hand in marriage.

The two of us had spent the afternoon retracing some of our favorite haunts and reliving some of our favorite memories. When we arrived back at the house, all five of my buddies were there to greet us. They were watching a baseball game, I think. When they left the room at my signal, I grabbed my guitar from its hiding place behind the TV and played and sang a song that ended with the words "Will you be my wife?" Then I got down on one knee and pulled the ring out from under the couch where Jess was sitting.

I heard a couple of my friends snickering in the hall when Jess pinned my arms to my chest with a hug so big I had trouble getting the ring on her finger. But then all five of them were cheering and high fiving each other. Before long, they were praying for my fiancée and me—pouring blessings over us and asking God to unite us in the strongest bonds of love. Then we brought out food and drinks and all celebrated for hours.

Maybe you don't see the appeal in having a group of guys hanging around and gawking at you during one of the more personal moments of your life. That's okay. I get that. But inviting my friends to participate in that happiest of moments was natural for me. It was instinctive. That's because the six of us had become more than ordinary friends. We were more like brothers—young men on the cusp of full adulthood, all connected at a deeper level by a shared experience of authentic Christian community.

Growing up, I was unfailingly attracted to superficial expressions of community, like sports teams, academic clubs, and youth groups. I enjoyed connecting with others through shared experiences, and I liked the idea of having friends—to a point. With very few exceptions, I preferred to keep relationships at a superficial level instead of looking for ways to go deeper.

That's why living in a house with five of my closest friends was transformational for me—and I try not to use the word *transformational* lightly. That year was a turning point that changed my life. Sure, in many ways we were a typical group of young, irresponsible guys still unsure of what it meant to live in the "real world." We spent a lot of time watching movies and playing video games. We didn't sleep much, usually because intense games of Monopoly demanded our attention into the early hours of the morning. We made fun of each other and played jokes on each other and shared a lot of frozen dinners.

But we also prayed for each other regularly and intensely. We gathered for shared devotions throughout the week—sometimes scheduled but often spontaneous. Several of us played guitar (at several different skill levels), and other people often heard the sound of our worship from the sidewalks outside. We confessed our sins to each other, we repented, and we requested accountability for that repentance because we wanted to become better men. Even more, we invited freshmen and sophomores from the school to participate in these activities with us; we tried to serve as mentors to the best of our ability.

In short, although we didn't realize it at the time, our house began to resemble the kind of community highlighted in Acts 2:42–47:

> They devoted themselves to the apostles' teaching and to fellowship, to the breaking of bread and to prayer. Everyone was filled with awe at the many wonders and signs performed by the apostles. All the believers were together and had everything in common. They sold property and possessions to give to anyone who had need. Every day they continued to meet together in the temple courts. They broke bread in their homes and ate together with glad and sincere hearts, praising God and enjoying the favor of all the people. And the Lord added to their number daily those who were being saved.

I consider that year spent "doing life together" with friends my first encounter with the modern phenomenon known as small groups. In many ways it was the best small group I've ever experienced; it was certainly the most intense. And when it ended, I wanted more.

Fortunately, once we were engaged, Jess and I were invited to participate in our church's small group for young couples. Then when the group leader and his wife moved to a different state several months after our wedding, we took his place.

That was my first official post as a small group leader, and the results were mixed. Yes, our group provided a place for young couples to build relationships and eventually put down roots within the broader congregation. Yes, many of us grew in our knowledge and understanding of God's Word. Yes, we learned a great deal about our spouses. We experienced a lot of positives (and a lot of fun!).

At the same time, however, those positive gains were continually derailed by a wide variety of distractions, including relational conflict and mistrust. The group suffered from a lack of direction and focus. Were we meeting every week to learn about the Bible? To form relationships? To pray? To become better wives and husbands? I don't think any of us were sure.

Worst of all, the members of the group—including me—were experiencing very little in the way of spiritual transformation. Certainly, when I compared the results of that group to the year I'd spent living in a true version of Christian community with those five guys, I felt like a failure—especially since I was the one who carried the title *leader*.

Looking back on that experience, what galls me most is that I could have solved the problems that kept knocking us off track if I'd been properly trained or taken the time to seek the advice of those more experienced in small group ministry. Thankfully, though, it wasn't long before I got a boost in my small group education.

My first "real" job was serving as an editor for Christianity Today International, which is how I got connected with a new website called SmallGroups.com. I managed that resource for more than five years, pouring myself into learning everything I could about small groups ministry and then using our platform to distribute what I learned to churches and group leaders around the world. I had the privilege of meeting with and learning from leading authorities on small groups and discipleship, and I enjoyed every opportunity to connect with regular group leaders working in the spiritual trenches of their communities.

After Christianity Today, I accepted a job with Lifeway Christian Resources in Nashville, Tennessee. When I was hired, Lifeway had just celebrated a hundred years of developing Sunday school curriculum and other resources for the church, which meant my education in small groups was just getting started. I spent a few years helping produce resources from many authors, including Tony Evans, Matt Chandler, David Platt, and Jen Hatmaker. I also served as the editor of *Bible Studies for Life*, which at the time was the largest curriculum resource in the history of the church.

After Lifeway, I stayed in Nashville to join HarperCollins Christian Publishing, which gave me the chance to work with spiritual giants such as David Jeremiah, Os Guinness, and Max Lucado. Talk about a dream come true!

Here's the point: I've spent almost twenty years of my life saturated in the world of Bible study and small groups from two distinct points of view. On the professional side, I've worked shoulder to shoulder with some of the best Bible teachers and curriculum developers on the planet. On the personal side, I've continued to invest myself in others through groups, Sunday school classes, and the ministry of the local church. I've taught teenagers, I've led couples, and I've served men and women of all ages.

In other words, I've spent the past two decades in an extended experiment with small groups and discipleship. I've learned a great deal about what works, what doesn't work, and why serving others in the context of community is worth every moment you can invest.

Now I'm passing those lessons on to you.

 Introduction

I've got good news and bad news for any current or potential group leader.

First, the good news: it's rare for people to have a totally negative experience during a small group gathering. Bad things do happen on occasion, of course. But it's unlikely you'll ever lead an unmitigated disaster of a group meeting where the majority of participants feel angry or cheated or wronged. I base that statement on two decades of personal experience with group gatherings, plus hundreds of conversations with group leaders and participants.

Small groups offer a chance for social interaction and relationships within a collection of (generally speaking) nice people in a culture where 25 percent of the population lacks even one close friend.[1] Even more, small groups are a venue for exploring the Bible—the bestselling book of all time—and its intersection with the troubles and triumphs of everyday life.

Sometimes you even get free food!

Now the bad news: even though it's uncommon for people to have a terrible experience during a group gathering, it's just as rare for group members to have an overwhelmingly positive experience—moving beyond the realm of polite get-togethers and surface conversations and justifying the continual investment of time and effort required by the leader and participants alike.

In other words, most people who participate in a small group don't experience life-change because of it. They don't experience transformation.

I know this because I've heard the stories. Throughout all my conversations with pastors and group leaders, one theme has popped up over and over again: "We like the idea of small groups, and we understand the basic format, but how do we get them to actually work?"

That's the question I tackle throughout this book, and my goals are simple.

I want your group to succeed—whether you're leading a couples group in your home, a Sunday school class at church, a Monday morning chat session with friends at a local coffee shop, a gathering of men at your local prison, or any other expression of biblical community. I want to help you make that expression *work*. I want you to talk with your spouse or your friend after a group meeting and say, "Wow. That went really, really well."

Importantly, I didn't write this book to help you launch a small groups ministry or recruit a dozen new leaders or develop a software solution to track group attendance over the course of months—or any other tasks typically associated with small groups at the church-wide level. Instead, these pages focus on one specific element of the small group experience: a group leader's responsibility to prepare for and lead group meetings.

To me, this responsibility is the cornerstone of a discipleship ministry. If group leaders can be successful in this task, their groups have an excellent chance of developing into spiritually healthy communities. And if groups are healthy, the small group ministry as a whole will be full of life. And if a church's small group ministry is thriving, that church will have a greater impact for the kingdom of God within its community. And on it goes.

So if you're a group leader, I believe your efforts at planning and leading your group week after week or month after month are of great importance. And I sincerely believe this book will help you take those experiences to the next level—specifically in terms of life-change and spiritual transformation.

I don't say this book will make leading a group easy for you. To prepare for and lead a group gathering, you need to function as at least a semi-expert in theology, discipleship, Christian education, worship, prayer, and interpersonal dynamics. That's a tall task! Which means it will never be as "easy as 1-2-3."

Still, making that process a bit easier is my goal in writing this book. I want to make sure your foundation as a leader is secure, and I want to equip you with a few tools (some basic, others more advanced) to help you maximize that hour or two spent with group members—and the chain of group meetings as they occur—in such a way that spiritual growth occurs and participants' lives are changed for the better. I want to help you prepare for and lead group meetings (or gatherings or whatever you call them) that won't just "work" but will be transformational.

Each chapter in this book will help you take a specific step toward that goal.

What's *not* here, by the way? Depending on your church's denomination or model of small group ministry, you may be asked to perform several (or even all) of the following tasks: recruiting group members, training an apprentice, tracking birthdays and anniversaries, arranging childcare, filing attendance reports, mentoring potential group leaders, planning social events—and more. All those tasks are important, and each of them can contribute to the overall health of a small group; I want to be clear about that. But those tasks are not a focus of this book, and I don't offer much advice about them.

First, it's usually best for group leaders to delegate some or even all those tasks to an apprentice or other members of the group. Doing so relieves some of the pressure the group leader can feel and empowers other participants to take ownership within the group, moving them to a deeper level of commitment. Second, several resources already provide helpful guidance for completing those tasks—especially SmallGroups.com.

One more thing—and this isn't really a goal as much as it's a request. The core idea behind this ministry we call "small groups" (or Sunday school or community discipleship or whatever term you prefer to use) is that disciples of Jesus are not meant to follow after Him alone. God is a divine community, and we are made in His image—created to live and learn and love and serve in community as well.

So here's my request: don't read this book alone if you can help it. Don't attempt to train yourself in how to lead a group as if this were a textbook and you have a quiz tomorrow morning. Rather, read this book in community with at least one other person. Read it with a mentor who has experience leading groups and can help you process what you learn. Read it with fellow group leaders who will be preparing for and leading group meetings alongside you. Talk about what you read within these pages. Discuss what you find helpful or confusing—or just plain weird.

Thank you for reading, and may God bless your faithful service.

I_ _____ _I _____ _I

Mapping the Terrain

If you've ever been to Walt Disney World, you know it's a great place for family fun. You also know it's really, really big—27,258 acres. That much space provides room for four theme parks, two water parks, four golf courses, thirty-six hotels, over one hundred restaurants, and an entire transportation system complete with highways, monorails, and canals. Whew!

That much space can be a nightmare when it comes to navigation.

These days, enthusiasts can use a helpful app on their phones to explore every nook and cranny of Disney World. The GPS feature shows you exactly where you are and gives you a helpful path to get wherever you want to go.

But I'm old enough to remember when visitors unfamiliar with Disney World had to rely on—gasp!—maps. They had two kinds back then. The first was a printed map you could carry with you. They displayed everything visitors could see in a particular park, right down to the restrooms and lemon ice vendors. But I found them unhelpful for two reasons. First, you needed an engineering degree to refold them. And second, they required complex triangulations to figure out where you happened to be standing at any particular moment.

That's why I preferred Disney's second type of map: the directories. Those were larger versions of the printed maps on free-standing kiosks spread throughout the several parks. But with one significant difference: each directory contained a red arrow with the words "You are here." Armed with the knowledge of where you were on the map, it was pretty easy to orient yourself and decide where you wanted to go next.

That's the goal of this part One. Whether you're a new group leader or a veteran of many years, I want to ensure you have a proper orientation when it comes to leading other people as part of a transformational, Christ-centered community. To do that, the first five chapters explore the important foundational elements of leading a group:

> ➤ Chapter 1 provides answers to basic questions: What is a small group? What are the primary purpose and essential activities of a group meeting? What is your role as "leader"?
> ➤ Chapter 2 reveals the biblical foundation for small groups and other expressions of biblical community. That foundation is discipleship.
> ➤ Chapter 3 explores the place of hospitality within your role as a group leader—because transformation requires a lot more than just information.
> ➤ Chapter 4 answers the question, "Are small groups still relevant?" In a world increasingly lived online and where social

media continues to explode, can community gatherings still benefit us? And is it possible to mesh discipleship with the internet in a way that's helpful? (Hint: the answer to all those questions is yes.)

➤ Chapter 5 addresses the important role learning styles can play in group discussions and the overall life of a community. Understanding the different ways people learn and grow is critical for serving everyone in a group.

Solidifying your grasp of the concepts in these next five chapters will give you that red arrow, like the one on Disney's directories. It will help you understand where you are and prepare you to move forward into an exciting experience for both you and your group.

Chapter 1

Small Groups 101

I think it's important to start by laying out some basic definitions and answering some foundational questions about this concept we call small groups.

Several different methods and models of small group ministry exist, which means there's no real consensus on the definition of a small group. Here's a definition I've found helpful over the years, and I think it fits the purposes of this book: *a small group is a collection of three to thirty people who regularly meet and participate in activities together with the goal of experiencing spiritual growth.*

A number of key terms need to be highlighted in that definition. First, I've limited a small group to "three to thirty people" because three people (rather than an individual or a pair) is the smallest number that can be considered a group. The upper number was harder to define. Many group practitioners believe an ideal group consists of six to ten people. It's possible, however, to deal with larger numbers by "subgrouping"—dividing the group into smaller subgroups for discussion, prayer, or other activities. At the same time, growing beyond thirty people pushes the boundaries on practical matters like finding enough chairs for everyone, parking, and maintaining relationships.

Next, it's important that a small group be defined as a collection of people who "regularly meet." Most groups meet once a week, although a number of groups remain healthy while gathering every two weeks or even once a month. This regular interaction is a key ingredient in the formation of what we often refer to as "community"—that state of being where a group of people form deeper relationships through regular interaction and a common purpose.

As the author of Hebrews writes, "Let us consider how we may spur one another on toward love and good deeds, not giving up meeting together, as some are in the habit of doing, but encouraging one another—and all the more as you see the Day approaching" (Heb. 10:24–25). In my opinion, it would be difficult for a group to maintain cohesion if the participants gathered less frequently than once a month—or if they met sporadically, without a regular schedule and defined intervals between each gathering.

Finally, members of a small group "participate in activities together with the goal of experiencing spiritual growth." People need to do stuff when they get together as a group. They need to take part in specific activities. And the ultimate goal of those activities is to help group members mature and develop as disciples of Jesus Christ. On the other side, those activities also help group members reject sin and elements of the world that would drag them away from Jesus Christ and thus limit their spiritual growth.

This echoes Peter's words to the early church: "Dear friends, since you have been forewarned, be on your guard so that you may not be carried away by the error of the lawless and fall from your secure position. But grow in the grace and knowledge of our Lord and Savior Jesus Christ. To him be glory both now and forever! Amen" (2 Peter 3:17–18).

What Is the Primary Purpose of a Group Meeting?

I briefly answered this earlier, but it's worth a bit of further exploration. The goal of a small group is spiritual growth. It's transformation.

It's helping participants move away from that first gasping breath they took as born-again children of God, still wallowing in their sin, and toward their ultimate identity as fully glorified disciples of Christ. (And if your group has evangelistic success, that also means seeing participants take that first breath as newly born children of God.)

Maybe you're thinking, *Isn't spiritual growth the goal of each Christian as an individual?* Yes it is. Anyone who follows Jesus as their Lord is supposed to be working toward becoming more like Him every day (see John 13:12–17). We have a lot of words for that process, like sanctification, spiritual growth, transformation, and life-change.

The thing is when I look back over my life, I see the least amount of spiritual growth during those times when I tried to go it alone. Just recently, for example, I had the chance to supervise the revision of a major study Bible. It was a freelance assignment, which meant I did most of my work during evenings and weekends. I spent a full year in verse-by-verse exploration of the Bible, and as part of the editing process, I read through and evaluated all seven thousand study notes—twice.

By the end of the project, I was a little sick of Bible verses, to be honest. And I had real trouble getting motivated to interpret and discuss portions of Scripture with my small group, let alone lead the process. So I withdrew. I pulled back from my group members. I didn't quit the group, but I isolated myself both inside and outside our group meetings. And I encountered consequences because of that isolation—damage to myself spiritually and damage to the progress of our group.

I like what Kevin Miller, a former vice president of *Christianity Today*, used to say during our planning meetings: "Spiritual growth never happens in a vacuum."

I also like how Paul highlights this idea in Ephesians 4, starting with verses 1–7:

As a prisoner for the Lord, then, I urge you to live a life worthy of the calling you have received. Be completely humble and gentle; be patient, bearing with one another in love. Make every effort to keep the unity of the Spirit through the bond of peace. There is one body and one Spirit, just as you were called to one hope when you were called; one Lord, one faith, one baptism; one God and Father of all, who is over all and through all and in all. But to each one of us grace has been given as Christ apportioned it.

After a little tangent regarding Christ's resurrection and ascension, Paul continues with verses 11–16:

So Christ himself gave the apostles, the prophets, the evangelists, the pastors and teachers, to equip his people for works of service, so that the body of Christ may be built up until we all reach unity in the faith and in the knowledge of the Son of God and become mature, attaining to the whole measure of the fullness of Christ.

Then we will no longer be infants, tossed back and forth by the waves, and blown here and there by every wind of teaching and by the cunning and craftiness of people in their deceitful scheming. Instead, speaking the truth in love, we will grow to become in every respect the mature body of him who is the head, that is, Christ. From him the whole body, joined and held together by every supporting ligament, grows and builds itself up in love, as each part does its work.

Notice how the individual and communal elements of the Christian life are interwoven throughout the passage. Christ equips *everyone* so that "the body of Christ may be built up" and "we all reach unity in the faith and in the knowledge of the Son of God and become mature, attaining to the whole measure of the fullness of Christ."

Personal sanctification is important, yes, but our growth in Christ as individuals is supplemented and boosted when we choose to work toward that goal as part of a community. This communal desire for spiritual growth should be the primary purpose of your group as a whole, and it should be the primary goal of each individual group meeting you lead.

I'm thankful for that communal approach and the blessings I've received through community. During my season of feeling oversaturated by Scripture—or more accurately, feeling oversaturated by studying what other people have written about Scripture—my group was patient with me. They stepped up when I needed to step back. And when that season passed, I was able to reengage with a deeper appreciation for not having to carry the full load as a leader.

What Are the Essential Activities of a Group Meeting?

So what happens in a small group that helps people achieve that primary goal of spiritual growth and transformation? The following is a list of what I consider the core practices the participants of a group should undertake when they gather.

Social connection and fellowship. Group members need time to hang out and enjoy one another's company. Doing so helps everyone form and maintain strong relationships, which is critical because the relational nature of small groups is what separates them from personal spiritual growth (as with daily devotions) and corporate events (like weekend worship services). Social interaction can and should happen outside of group meetings as well.

Interaction with God's Word. I don't think small groups should avoid topical discussions or that every group meeting needs to be a straight-out Bible study. The Bible, however, needs to be the primary source of truth for a small group, and that source needs to be accessed and examined habitually. In

Jesus's words, "If you hold to my teaching, you are really my disciples. Then you will know the truth, and the truth will set you free" (John 8:31–32). Without the foundation of Scripture, a small group devolves into a Kiwanis Club or group therapy at a psychologist's office—usually minus the psychologist.

Group discussion. The exchange of ideas is an important element within a small group—offering opinions, asking questions, sharing interpretations, expressing confusion. This includes discussion about the Bible but other topics and ideas as well. Without this "iron sharpens iron" aspect, a small group becomes a lecture in a classroom.

Learning activities. I know *learning activities* is a broad term, but I use it in reference to the educational elements of a group meeting that go beyond discussion. This includes icebreakers, object lessons, role playing, and games. These elements are important because they appeal to group members with various learning styles and preferences.

Prayer. Approaching God through prayer has always been a core practice of Jesus's disciples, both as individuals and communities. Indeed, the New Testament is bursting with commands about prayer written to the members of the early church. "Do not be anxious about anything, but in every situation, by prayer and petition, with thanksgiving, present your requests to God" is a good example (Phil. 4:6). So is 1 Thessalonians 5:16–18: "Rejoice always, pray continually, give thanks in all circumstances; for this is God's will for you in Christ Jesus."

Worship. Worship is an appropriate response to our interaction with God and His Word during a group meeting. And it should be noted that worship in a group can incorporate music and singing, but it doesn't have to. Other expressions of worship include contemplation, *Lectio Divina*, Scripture reading, liturgical prayer, and physical movement.

Application. I like what Eugene Peterson wrote about applying God's Word: "The most important question we ask of this text is not, 'What does this mean?' but 'What can I obey?' A simple act of obedience will open up our lives to this text far more quickly than any number of Bible studies and dictionaries and concordances."[1] The best group meetings include interacting with and discussing God's Word, but they don't stop there; they move toward application. Sometimes that means discussing how group members can apply lessons learned in their individual lives, and other times this involves group members getting off their seats and taking action together.

One more thing: it's important to note that group leaders don't have to shoehorn all these activities into every one of their gatherings—nor do they have to make sure each element receives equal time. It's appropriate to spend a group meeting entirely in prayer, for example (or discussion, application, or fellowship). It would also be appropriate to defer worship and learning activities if a group member required an extended time of prayer.

What Is Your Primary Role as a Group Leader?

If the purpose of a small group and its meetings is spiritual growth for everyone participating, how does the group leader fit into that process? How do we lead other people in a way that results in spiritual transformation?

Those are important questions. Unfortunately, I believe they've been answered incorrectly by many church leaders and ministry directors. And as a result, a large percentage of small group leaders in the Western church suffer from an identity crisis.

Here's a quick question to show you what I mean: What label does your church currently use to describe your ministry role?

Group leader? Host? Facilitator? Shepherd? Are you part of a life group, a home group, a connection group, a community group—or something completely different? I've encountered each of these terms over the years, and I usually see a new one on a church website every few months.

On the one hand, it's not a big deal that different churches use their own terminology to describe the same ministry role. People have diverse ways of expressing themselves. Church leaders emphasize one word over another as a way of prioritizing specific functions or tasks. It's to be expected. On the other hand, this wide variety of ministry titles can be viewed as a symptom of the larger identity crisis affecting group ministries today.

Put simply, many group leaders in today's churches don't have a firm grasp on what their role is supposed to be, which means they don't have a firm grasp on the goals they're trying to accomplish, which means they don't have a firm grasp at all about what they're supposed to be doing in their groups.

This identity crisis manifests itself in two ways. First, group leaders suffer from a lack of focus. When they don't have a clear focus regarding their ministry role, they often wander. They become like ships without a rudder, drifting from one current to the next.

That's a bad thing for group leaders and group members alike. When people attempt to lead others without clarity and confidence, the result is a hesitant exploration of truth and stunted spiritual formation for all involved—and that's the best-case scenario. At worst, group leaders suffering from a lack of focus can unwittingly pilot their groups toward heresy, apathy, bitterness, or a destructive combination of all three.

Second, group leaders suffer from a misguided focus. Many group leaders have an idea about their ministry role that's both practical and well-defined but also inaccurate. In other words, they have a strong focus, but they're pointed in the wrong direction. This can happen when a church actively points its group leaders the wrong way, or when group leaders choose their own focus after drifting for a while in the already-mentioned scenario.

This second manifestation of the identity crisis is especially damaging because it's so subtle and insidious. It's entirely possible for you as a group leader to genuinely care for the people in your group, to be dedicated in your ministry role, to research all the latest tips about group dynamics and interpersonal relationships, and yet lead your group gatherings in a way that results in little or no spiritual fruit. And all because you were pointed in the wrong direction from the beginning.

So let me identify several of the "wrong directions" common in small group ministries today. Generally speaking, a group leader should not be defined *primarily* as any of the following when it comes to leading others during group meetings.

Teacher. You've probably encountered a "lecturer" in a group, whether this person was the group leader or a member. They monopolized everyone's time by spewing out facts and opinions one after another. And that's a bad idea. We know that.

But I intentionally use the word *teacher* here in order to highlight an important misconception: many group leaders believe their primary role is that of a teacher. They think the group is successful if the people involved are learning facts and ideas about God, the Bible, and the world—especially if those people can regurgitate those facts. But that's not the case. It's possible to comprehend all kinds of spiritual doctrines and ideas yet remain spiritually stagnant.

As group leaders, we must understand that it's entirely possible to be an excellent teacher—not a "lecturer" but someone who genuinely helps people learn during group meetings—and yet still fail to help our group members become more like Jesus Christ. As Paul said, "Knowledge puffs up while love builds up" (1 Cor. 8:1).

Facilitator. Many churches want their group leaders to think of themselves as facilitators rather than leaders. This is to combat the "group leader as lecturer" problem mentioned above, or to prevent people from claiming the title of *leader* and lording it over the other members of the group. But this approach creates several problems of its own. Just as viewing group leaders primarily as teachers elevates information over transformation, viewing them as facilitators elevates discussion over transformation. The group is deemed successful if people experience good conversation and a high level of participation rather than basing the criteria for success on interaction with the Holy Spirit resulting in spiritual growth.

Host. Host has become a popular redefinition of what it means to be a group leader in recent years, primarily due to the influence of video curriculum. The idea is that a person or couple can host a group in their home, pop in a DVD or scan a streaming code, and let a "professional" manage the task of leading the group into meaningful experiences with God and His Word.

But one major flaw is inherent in this method of "leading" a small group: a video can't respond to the movement of the Holy Spirit. A pre-recorded speaker can't care for people or provide targeted encouragement and support. So what happens when a group member is convicted of sin during the discussion and begins weeping? Who calls the group to prayer when a couple mentions they're in danger of losing their house or their marriage? These situations require a leader. And that leader is supposed to be you.

My point is this: video Bible studies and other curriculum materials can be a helpful item in your toolbox as a group leader, but they can't replace *you*.

Another group member. Ironically, many church leaders don't like the term *leader*. They discourage their group leaders from acting differently than group members because they want to communicate that group members are just as important and valuable as group leaders—which is true. But being equal in terms of worth and value doesn't mean people have to adopt the same roles and functions. The reality is that a group with no leader will rarely move forward.

Let me be clear about one thing before moving on: I'm not saying group leaders should avoid demonstrating any of these important qualities. Quite the opposite. Group leaders should be able to facilitate discussions, host a gathering, and teach when necessary. Those are important and necessary skills. What I am saying is that group leaders go wrong when they make any of these skills the primary focus of their role within their groups.

Okay, now we're back to that important question: How do we lead a group meeting in a way that results in spiritual growth? What is the primary role of a group leader?

Let's start with another definition: *a group leader prepares for group meetings, both short-term and long-term, and leads group members through the essential activities of those meetings in submission to the Holy Spirit.*

First is the necessity of *preparation*. Group leaders are charged with scheduling the essential activities performed by the group, like social interaction, discussion, prayer, and worship to name a few. Group leaders also perform research or acquire supplies as necessary to help the group get the most out of those activities.

This preparation occurs both in the short-term and long-term. As a group leader, you'll set the agenda and prepare an activity for the meeting coming up this Wednesday, but you'll also keep a loose plan in place for the five other meetings to take place before Easter. (I'll go into greater detail on how to prepare for a group meeting in Part Two.)

The next word is important: a group leader *leads*. Simply put, you need to embrace your role as a leader within your group. That doesn't mean you're more valuable than the other group members, but it does mean your role is set apart from theirs. When someone in the group needs to make a decision, offer guidance, provide clarity, or choose a direction, that person needs to be you.

More, a group leader needs to *lead group members*. The people within your group are unique individuals with unique strengths, weaknesses, needs, and gifts. That means you'll be most effective as a leader when you tailor the elements of a group meeting to maximize those strengths and gifts—and to address those areas of weakness and need. It's also important to have an idea of how your group members are coming together as a group. They're not a collection of individuals attempting spiritual growth separately; they're a community of people growing together.

For these reasons and more, you need to get to know your group members within the context of genuine relationships. You can't lead well if you remain isolated from the people following you.

The final phrase is important: *in submission to the Holy Spirit*. A small group gathering is more than a collection of ordinary activities and rituals performed by people. The goal of these meetings is spiritual growth, which makes them spiritual in nature. In fact, it makes them supernatural. That means they require the presence and impact of the Holy Spirit in order to be successful.

Now it's time for a little metaphor.

Group Leaders as Spiritual Safari Guides

Imagine the following scenario: You're going on a safari. You've done extensive research and chosen the perfect wilderness organization to help you come face-to-face with elephants or crocodiles or monkeys or exotic birds—whatever series of God's creatures really gets your fire going. Sure it's expensive, but this is a once-in-a-lifetime experience. You're totally excited.

You purchase tickets to Africa or maybe South America, and you have a great experience on the flight. You've packed lots of new survival clothing and high-tech wilderness gadgets, and by some miracle all your luggage arrives at the same airport as you—and at the same time. The trip couldn't be going better.

Pretty soon you're riding in a jeep with four other adventurers. Your safari guide is driving. His name is Crush, or something cool like that, and he speaks perfect English. He looks rugged and dependable—capable of thriving in the wild and helping others do the same. Plus, he's wearing the same kind of hat Crocodile Dundee wore in that late 1980s movie you really liked.

When everyone gets out of the Jeep, you're standing on the threshold of an untamed jungle. You see huge trees with exotic leaves and hanging vines. You smell the light perfume of wild blossoms mixed with the musty scent of bark and fungus and dirt. You hear the bubbling of a river somewhere off to your left and the frantic, continuous call of unknown birds.

Then it all begins to go off track.

First, Crush pulls a folding chair from the back of the Jeep, then opens it and sits down. He takes off his hat and says, "Everyone gather round. Circle up on me." Crush takes out a large notebook and starts talking about the jungle behind you. He talks for more than half an hour. He tells a few stories about his experiences in the jungle and reads some interesting facts out of his notebook—at least, they'd be interesting if you weren't standing in front of the real thing.

When Crush closes his notebook, he asks if anyone has any questions about what he just shared. No one does. Then he asks several questions of his own. He wants to know if anyone has ever been in a jungle, and if so, what it was like. He wants to know how you all react emotionally to the idea of a jungle—are you more afraid or interested? He wants you to repeat some of the facts he read out of the notebook. Sometimes he just rereads different sections when nobody seems to remember the right answer.

After a particularly long and awkward silence, Crush looks down at his watch and says, "Hey, it's getting late. We better pray and head back." Crush closes his eyes and thanks God for a safe drive out to the jungle and the chance to have a "good discussion." Then everyone piles back into the Jeep, and off you go.

Not a very satisfying safari, huh?

The reason is obvious: your leader had a poor understanding of what he was supposed to do. He helped you get close to the jungle. He gave you some interesting information. He gave you a chance to talk with the other people in the group. But he never took you where you wanted to go. He never helped you experience anything.

That's a poor way to approach a safari, and that's a poor way to approach a group meeting. Yet it happens every week in countless groups across America and around the world. Why? Because group leaders have a poor understanding of their role when it comes to leading others. They think they're supposed to act mainly as teachers or hosts or facilitators—or something else entirely.

If you're a small group leader (or a Sunday school teacher or fill another similar role), I encourage you to think of yourself as a spiritual safari guide. Your job is not to help people memorize interesting facts about God, the Bible, or church history. Your job is not to get people to debate those interesting facts. Your job is not to provide a comfortable place for people to do the debating.

No, your job is to lead your group members into direct encounters with the life-changing truths written into every page of God's Word—like faith and sin and hope and temptation and love. Your job is to help your group members grapple with those truths, understand how those truths intersect with their stories, and then make decisions and take actions based on those truths.

Again, I've written this book to provide you with some basic principles and tools, which will help you operate as a spiritual safari guide. But you need to keep one more thing in mind as you do.

It's All about the Holy Spirit

As you prepare to carry out your role as a spiritual safari guide, remember this: you can't manufacture spiritual growth within your group members (or within yourself, actually). No matter how good you become at leading discussion or prayer or worship or application, you can't force your group members to grow spiritually any more than you can force them to grow taller.

The reality is that spiritual growth and transformation occur only through the supernatural work of the Holy Spirit. Jesus says a lot about this process in John 14–16, especially this passage:

> Unless I go away, the Advocate will not come to you; but if I go, I will send him to you. When he comes, he will prove the world to be in the wrong about sin and righteousness and judgment: about sin, because people do not believe in me; about righteousness, because I am going to the Father, where you can see me no longer; and about judgment, because the prince of this world now stands condemned.
>
> I have much more to say to you, more than you can now bear. But when he, the Spirit of truth, comes, he will guide you into all the truth. (John 16:7–13)

At first glance, that idea seems at odds with everything I've written up to this point. I mean, think about these two statements:

1. A group leader's primary job is to prepare for and lead group meetings that result in spiritual growth.
2. Spiritual growth can be achieved only through the work of the Holy Spirit.

Those ideas almost seem mutually exclusive, right? If group leaders are charged with striving for a goal only the Holy Spirit can fulfill, how can we lead well?

The answer is relatively simple: group leaders need to lead their group meetings in such a way that the members are able to connect with the Holy Spirit.

One of the best ways to understand this is to think about falling asleep. You can't force yourself to fall asleep. No matter how hard you try, no mental or physiological switch you can flick in order to slip into unconsciousness exists. But you can create an environment that's conducive to sleep. You can turn off the lights, get a soft pillow, wear comfortable clothes, and (if you're like me) turn on a little white noise.

Achieving transformation in your small group follows a similar dynamic. You can't force your group members to humbly seek the Holy Spirit. You can't compel the Holy Spirit to convict anyone of their sin or move into your group with a rushing wind and tongues of fire. But you can create an environment within your group meetings conducive to regular, life-changing encounters with the Holy Spirit—which is exactly what I mean when I talk about being a spiritual safari guide.

Chapter 2

The Ministry of Discipleship

Have you noticed the world seems heavy with questions but light on answers? Sadly, we'll never find an answer to so many of those questions.

Here are some examples:

> Why is lemon juice made with artificial flavoring while dishwashing liquid is made with real lemons?
> Why is *abbreviated* such a long word?
> Why doesn't glue stick to the inside of the bottle?
> Why do airplanes have flotation devices under their seats instead of parachutes?

Okay, enough silly stuff. When used correctly, *Why?* is one of the most important questions we can ask about the most important priorities in our lives. It cuts through our actions and highlights our motivations. It forces us to evaluate the impulses and values at the heart of what we do.

So before we go any further, let's take a quick step back and use that critical question to evaluate this concept we call small groups. Why should you and I be involved in small groups or Sunday school classes or whatever phrase we use to describe gathering in community? Why should we lead those groups? Why should we invest our time, talent, and treasure in the practice of gathering with other believers?

Those questions have many long answers, but I like the short answer best: discipleship.

The primary goal driving small groups in the church today is not fellowship. It's not Christian education. It's not accountability. It's not spiritual disciplines. It's not worship or prayer or service or any of the other important work that can be found in a typical group gathering. Yes, each of those elements is important for a successful group experience, but none are the key motivator.

Instead, the main goal of small groups, both individually and corporately, is to make disciples of Jesus Christ.

Now, the idea of "making" disciples has two important facets. The first is evangelism. Small groups and other intimate expressions of Christian community are an ideal place for people to encounter Jesus and accept His free gift of salvation. Groups offer an environment where people can hear the truth of God's Word, evaluate that truth through conversation, and learn how to respond through the examples of others.

The second facet of making disciples within the context of small groups is what I mentioned so often in chapter 1: spiritual formation. In my mind, small groups are the premier setting for disciples of Jesus to progress as disciples of Jesus—to grow and develop and mature.

These are the themes I explore in this chapter. Specifically, I want to give you a biblical foundation for your role as a group leader by exploring Jesus's Great Commission in greater detail, by looking through some of the great examples of disciple-makers in Scripture—and how their stories contribute to your understanding of what it means to lead a group—and by listing some of the great rewards you and I can experience when we invest ourselves in this important work.

The Great Commission

I often forget that Jesus's disciples received the Great Commission during a period of time both super exciting and super unsettling. It was exciting because of everything they'd seen and experienced in the weeks prior to that moment. Jesus had been crucified, but then He rose from the grave! They'd seen Him, heard Him, and even touched Him. But it was unsettling because Jesus appeared only in short bursts, which left the disciples huddled together much of the time, trying to figure out how to live and what was coming next when their own religious leaders were hostile to everything they believed.

I think that's why, when Jesus met His followers on that mountain near Jerusalem, the text says, "When they saw him, they worshiped him; but some doubted" (Matt. 28:17).

In response to that very human mixture of worship and doubt, Jesus delivered the mission priorities that have defined the church for two thousand years:

> Then Jesus came to them and said, "All authority in heaven and on earth has been given to me. Therefore go and make disciples of all nations, baptizing them in the name of the Father and of the Son and of the Holy Spirit, and teaching them to obey everything I have commanded you. And surely I am with you always, to the very end of the age." (vv. 18–20)

"Make disciples of all nations." That is our mission as followers of Jesus. When we followers of Jesus struggle with questions about purpose or ask *What am I supposed to do with my life?* we have at least one definitive answer: make disciples.

Notably, that command applies to all followers of Jesus. Pastors are commanded to make disciples. Lawyers are commanded to make disciples. Teachers are commanded to make disciples. Plumbers are commanded to make disciples. Stay-at-home moms and dads are commanded to make disciples. Yes, even kids and teenagers who are disciples of Jesus are commanded to make disciples.

That is our commission at home, at school, at work, at play—at all times. You and I are called to make disciples of all nations in obedience to our Lord, Jesus Christ.

That's why I'm thrilled you've made the decision (or are at least considering making the decision) to lead a group, teach a Sunday school class, mentor new Christians, or otherwise invest yourself in small expressions of Christian community. Because those groups are a wonderful setting for you to obey Jesus's command to make disciples.

Let's explore what that looks like a little more by focusing on the three complementary verbs in Jesus's Great Commission: *go, baptize, and teach.*

GO

Making disciples is an active practice, which I think is why Jesus started His commission with the emphatic word *go.*

Unfortunately, many followers of Jesus today have a passive approach to disciple-making. In many ways, we've outsourced that responsibility to the "professionals" at church. When we encounter neighbors or coworkers or friends who have the potential to grow spiritually, our typical first response is to take them to church. Then we expect our pastors and staff members to take it from there.

Of course, it doesn't help that pastors and churches often reinforce this outsourcing mentality. How many churches rev up their evangelism campaigns by bringing in guest speakers and encouraging members to "invite your friends to church"? How often do we promote the myth that something magical happens within the walls of a church sanctuary that can't happen in other places?

Just to be clear, there's nothing wrong with attending church or taking new people to your local congregation. But that in and of itself is not a biblical model for discipleship.

Worse, it's not a sustainable model. Why? Because real estate is expensive, building projects require a lot of investment, and even the largest church campuses can hold only a tiny portion of the population of the cities or communities in which they reside.

The truth is discipleship is bigger than churches. Which is why Jesus told us to "go."

Whereas church ministry is static and somewhat inflexible, groups ministry is the opposite. You can have a small group in your home, which is a great option. But you can also lead a small group at your local park. Or at your favorite coffee shop. Or in the break room at your office. Or at school. Or as many discovered during the dark years of the COVID-19 pandemic, you can lead a group online through video.

Small groups allow you to connect with potential disciples where they are, without the sometimes stigma of "attending church." They can be formal or informal, casual or committed, spontaneous or planned, short or brief.

In short, groups allow us to go. They give us a tool to make disciples in any context, which means we can obey our mission wherever we happen to be.

BAPTIZE

As I mentioned earlier, evangelism is a key facet to making disciples. Really, evangelism should be our key motivator when it comes to obeying the Great Commission. Every day we encounter people who don't have a saving relationship with Jesus Christ. Whether they are acquaintances or fast friends or even members of our own family, the reality is they all have incredible value as eternal beings created in God's image. They all have the opportunity to experience eternal life with God.

They just need to hear the truth. Which is where you and I come in—and where small groups can be a wonderful tool.

"Hey, Jeff, why don't you come to church with me on Sunday?" If you've ever started a conversation with that type of sentence, you know it's a big ask. A lot of cultural and social weight is attached to the idea of "attending church." A lot of potential baggage.

Here's a fact that might surprise you: only about 22 percent of Americans attend church every week. On the flip side, 56 percent seldom or never go to church—which is more than half of Americans.[1] So inviting someone to join you at church has increasingly become inviting someone to do something most people don't do. Something many people see as a little weird.

Contrast that "Come to church" invitation with these alternative options:

> "Hey, Jeff, some of us are gathering in the conference room during lunch to pray about the war. Care to join us?"

> "Hey, Jeff, three other guys and I meet after our workout every Thursday morning to help each other grow as dads. Wanna come?"

> "Hey, Jeff, a couples group meets in our home every other Monday night. We have dinner and then study something interesting from the Bible. What if you and your wife joined us next time?"

Beyond the act of inviting, group settings are helpful for the process of evangelism because they give us an opportunity to have deep, meaningful conversations without a public audience. Yes, there's power in "walking down the aisle" of a church to accept Christ, but that kind of invitation can also present a tremendous barrier.

The intimacy and relational trust that often develops in a group setting offers a wonderful environment for the Holy Spirit to grab hold of people through conviction, and it's a wonderful venue for people's questions to be asked and answered before, during, and after the process we call salvation.

Here's the good news for churches: the evangelistic benefits of group gatherings often come around full circle. When new believers are given the chance to grow and thrive in the smaller pond of a caring group, they eventually migrate into the bigger pond of church attendance. So groups don't need to be a replacement for the traditional church experience. When done well, they become a helpful and productive supplement.

TEACH

Have you seen how World War II fighter pilots drew little pictures on the outside of their jets to show how many "kills" they'd scored? That's often how it seems churches and Christians in general approach their efforts with evangelism. Once a person is saved, we check them off our list, encourage them to become church members, and move on to the next "target."

What a missed opportunity! Salvation isn't just the end of our old way of life; it's the beginning of something new—something wonderful. But that new life does need to be cultivated in order to grow.

In my experience, that's where groups shine. Groups are the ideal environment to help disciples of Jesus move from where they are spiritually to where they want to be spiritually. They give us opportunities to both identify and take our next steps—and to help and support and encourage others in doing the same.

The main reason groups are such powerful venues for spiritual growth and transformation is that they provide an opportunity for two-way communication.

When you think about it, our typical experiences at church almost always go one way. The pastor speaks, and we listen. The pastor gives, and we receive. There's value in those experiences, for sure. Much can be gained from faithful church attendance and "sitting at the feet" of a gifted teacher.

But when we gather in smaller expressions of community, we have the chance to talk together. Two ways. Everyone giving and everyone receiving. We can ask questions and work together to find answers. We can experiment and share our results. We can show others some steps to take through one-on-one modeling.

For all those reasons and many more, small groups help obey Jesus's commission to "teach" disciples how to live as disciples. And that potential for the spiritual transformation of individuals really opens the door for the secret ingredient of Christian discipleship: multiplication.

Think about it. If you faithfully lead a group for a year, chances are good that two of your group members may feel equipped to lead groups of their own the next year. Both of those groups can produce one or two more—meaning more groups—and then each of those groups can produce more groups, and on it goes. There's a real potential for explosive and exponential spiritual growth in a community when we do groups well.

Einstein supposedly said compound interest is the most powerful force in the universe. Well, compounding transformation may well be the most powerful force in the church.

Great Examples

We've seen that making disciples is our first command as followers of Jesus, and we've seen that small groups are a fantastic venue for obeying that command. But what does it actually mean to "make disciples"? What does that look like on a practical level?

The first way to answer that question is to review your own journey as a disciple of Jesus. What has helped you most in your spiritual transformation? Maybe more to the point, *who* has helped you most, and what steps or actions did those people take to facilitate your understanding of what it means to follow Christ?

Beyond our own experiences, though, we can benefit from several great examples of disciple-makers in God's Word. First and foremost, of course, is Jesus.

Quick question: How many disciples did Jesus have during His public ministry? Most people say twelve when I ask that question, but that's not correct. There were twelve "apostles," yes, but at times hundreds of people followed Jesus and considered themselves His disciples. These were part of the "crowds" that followed Him around from place to place and region to region.

Jesus spent time with those crowds—teaching, healing, correcting, and more. But not for all of His time or even most of His time. Instead, He selected twelve men with whom He invested Himself in a deeper relationship. And even among those twelve, Jesus gave extra attention or mentoring to three individuals: Peter, James, and John (see Matthew 7:1–13, for example).

In other words, Jesus was a small group leader. He didn't try to "change the world" by making Himself broadly available to the whole world and broadcasting His message from coast to coast. Rather, He invested Himself in a small number of men. He mentored the apostles by not just telling them the truth and telling them what to do but by showing them. He modeled what it meant to have an authentic, growing relationship with the Father. And He helped those in His group learn how to do what He did.

Then those apostles changed the world. Because, remember, small groups are a force for spiritual multiplication.

Think about some of the most significant moments in Jesus's ministry:

> Jesus calming the storm (Matt. 8:23–27)
> His instructions before sending out the apostles to minister in pairs (Matt. 10)
> His explanations of His parables (Mark 4:34)
> Jesus walking on water (Matt. 14:22–36)
> Peter's declaration that Jesus is the Messiah (Matt. 16:13–20)
> The transfiguration (Matt. 17:1–13)

> The last supper (Matt. 26:17–30)
> Prayer in the garden of Gethsemane (Matt. 26:36–46)
> Jesus's ascension (Acts 1:1–11).

Each of those incidents and many more took place in an intimate setting rather than in a public forum. In other words, they were each a part of Jesus's work as a small group leader discipling His group members.

Here's an interesting exercise: the next time you read one of the Gospels, do so through the lens of Jesus as a group leader. It really does change the way you see His life and ministry, and it can provide you with a wonderful example for how to make disciples in your world and your context today.

Speaking of other great examples, do you know who else functioned as a group leader in the New Testament? Paul did. And Peter. And John. And pretty much all the apostles and early church leaders.

One reason that's true is because nearly all the churches in the New Testament era were house churches. Once the early Christians experienced pushback and persecution from the religious leaders of their local synagogues, they gathered more frequently in one another's homes. Which means when you read about Paul planting churches in Ephesus or Colossae or those other cities of the ancient world, he was really planting a network of groups. When he identified leaders like Timothy and Silas as well as others on his missionary journeys, he established them as group leaders.

Just like you.

Don't skip past that reality. When you assume the mantle of a group leader, you're joining a movement that stretches back thousands of years. You don't have to be a pastor to join that movement. You don't have to be a spiritual giant or even someone who "has it all together." You just need to invest yourself in others. You just need to create a place where people, yourself included, can experience God, hear the truth, and support one another in obeying God's will.

That's discipleship. And that's the opportunity in front of you right now.

Great Rewards

Let's circle back to my original questions at the start of this chapter. Why invest your time, talent, and treasure in a small group? Why become a group leader?

Because doing so will contribute to the kingdom of God. Because you will grow spiritually, and you'll have the privilege of seeing others grow spiritually. Because you'll have fun. Because you'll find opportunities to form deep, life-changing friendships, and because you'll contribute to others finding the blessing of deep, life-changing friendships. Because you'll learn new things about God and His Word. Because you'll learn new things about yourself. Because you'll help others learn new things and apply them in ways that compound and expand everything I said above.

And because you'll be obeying God.

That's why.

Over the years, my wife and I have had the privilege of connecting with hundreds of people through the ministry of small groups, Sunday school classes, and more. We've seen marriages begin and end. We've seen children burst into the world and flourish. We've seen members of our groups serve our community in dozens of ways, including starting groups of their own. We've seen group members serve the world through missions from Haiti to Palestine to downtown Chicago.

Your story will be different. Your groups and your experiences will be unique to you. But I'm confident the end result will be the same: by leading groups, you will glorify God with your faithful and obedient service, and you will be blessed.

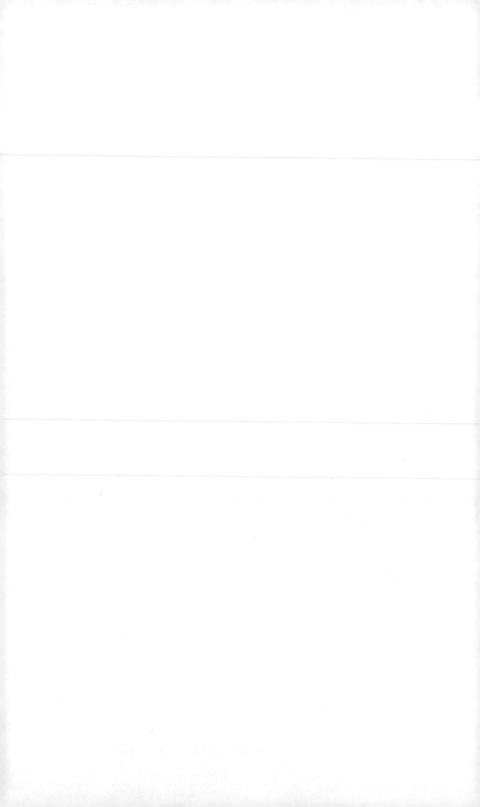

Chapter 3

The Ministry of Hospitality

Dr. Will Miller and Dr. Glenn Sparks authored *Refrigerator Rights: Creating Connections and Restoring Relationships*. The book explores the loss of intimate relationships in our modern culture, citing three primary culprits: increased mobility, a heavy social emphasis on individualism, and emotionally numbing distractions such as television and the internet.[1]

And that was before social media!

Miller was a noted psychotherapist at Purdue University at the time of the book's initial publication, and it was well received in sociological circles. And because Miller was (and still is) a popular speaker and an outspoken Christian, the book also received a lot of attention from church leaders—especially those interested in the world of small groups.

Here's how Miller describes this concept of "refrigerator rights":

> Refrigerator Rights Relationships are people who can open your refrigerator without having to ask permission. And when you are in their home you can do the same. They are people with whom you feel open, cared for, and relaxed. They know the real you

behind the facade. Such relationships are critical to a healthy life. Having "Refrigerator Rights" with someone means that you have a lifestyle that is connected and engaged. This is what too many of us are missing and yet what is necessary for a well-balanced life.[2]

I need to be honest about something here: I have never been able to establish refrigerator rights for myself with anyone outside of my family. I've actually stood in front of three different refrigerators, trying to psych myself up to take the plunge and open the door—but to no avail. All three times I shrank back and asked, "Can I grab a drink?"

Oh well. It may be that I have yet to experience the depth of relationship Miller describes. Or maybe I'm a private person and the idea of "refrigerator rights" is more of a helpful symbol than a practical benchmark. Either way, the concept highlights an important part of your ministry as a group leader: hospitality.

In this chapter, we'll explore how the following facets of hospitality can help you prepare for and lead small group meetings that result in spiritual growth:

> the role of chores in hospitality
> the role of prayer in hospitality
> the necessary element of fun

One more thing: I wrote this chapter under the assumption that the group leaders who read it are the primary hosts for their group meetings. That's a common practice in small groups, but other methods also work well. So if your group has a separate leader and host, or if your group rotates host locations (including meeting in public spaces), then this chapter will benefit both the group leader and anyone who participates in the ministry of hospitality by hosting the group.

The Role of Chores in Hospitality

I used to think of hospitality in terms of tasks to be completed before a group meeting, like vacuuming the rug, washing (or stashing) any dirty dishes, cleaning the bathroom, and baking cookies. And since I don't have much affinity or affection for those tasks, I viewed hospitality as a kind of necessary evil to be scratched off the list before I could move on to the more important work of finalizing discussion questions or preparing a prayer list.

I have repented of that mindset.

One reason for this repentance was my early work with SmallGroups.com, which brought me into contact with several people who have a more mature view on the topic. I was confronted, for example, with this explanation of hospitality written by Stephanie Voiland Rische:

> Hospitality isn't really about the physical interactions around the table with food and flatware settings (although those things certainly have their place). On a deeper level, it's more about the spiritual transactions that occur within the context of a shared home or a common meal. By this I don't necessarily mean evangelism, although that may be part of it. More than that, I want the people who cross the threshold of my home to experience a taste of Christ before they leave: a word of encouragement, a listening grace, the warmth of acceptance, an attempt at unconditional love.[3]

Another reason for my repentance is the overwhelming evidence in Scripture that hospitality is a vital ministry that goes way beyond vacuuming and picking up my kids' toys off the floor.

Think of all the significant events in the Old Testament preceded by an act of hospitality, involving Abraham and Melchizedek (Gen. 14:18–20), Rebekah and Abraham's servant (Gen. 24:12–27), Moses and Zipporah (Ex. 2:16–22), David and Abigail (1 Sam. 25:1–44), Elisha and the Shunammite woman (2 Kings 4:8–37)—and many others. Think also of Jesus's many instructions on the subject of hospitality. Like this one from Luke 14:12–14:

> Then Jesus said to his host, "When you give a luncheon or dinner, do not invite your friends, your brothers or sisters, your relatives, or your rich neighbors; if you do, they may invite you back and so you will be repaid. But when you give a banquet, invite the poor, the crippled, the lame, the blind, and you will be blessed. Although they cannot repay you, you will be repaid at the resurrection of the righteous."

Or what about this succinct promise from Him? "Truly I tell you, anyone who gives you a cup of water in my name because you belong to the Messiah will certainly not lose their reward" (Mark 9:41).

And then there's this command to His disciples, which seems to foreshadow some pretty serious consequences for people who refuse to demonstrate hospitality:

> Do not get any gold or silver or copper to take with you in your belts—no bag for the journey or extra shirt or sandals or a staff, for the worker is worth his keep. Whatever town or village you enter, search there for some worthy person and stay at their house until you leave. As you enter the home, give it your greeting. If the home is deserving, let your peace rest on it; if it is not, let your peace return to you. If anyone will not welcome you or listen to your words, leave that home or town and shake the dust off your feet. Truly I tell you, it will be more bearable for Sodom and Gomorrah on the day of judgment than for that town. (Matt. 10:9–15)

Here's my point: over and over again, hospitality in the Bible is presented as a catalyst for the movement of God and for spiritual growth in the lives of His people. I think it's vital for group leaders to understand this, because I believe spiritual growth is the primary purpose for groups and group meetings.

It's also vital for group leaders to understand that the root of hospitality—as presented in these Scriptures and other Bible passages—is an attitude of service and self-sacrifice. It's a willingness to offer our time, money, energy, food, and even our homes in an effort to love our neighbors as ourselves.

Yes, that attitude is often fleshed out through performing tasks—especially in the context of group meetings. I want to be clear that cleaning or vacuuming or setting the thermostat at a comfortable temperature isn't wrong; it's good. But there is a difference between task-oriented hospitality and biblical hospitality. There's a difference between cleaning the bathroom as an act of service and cleaning the bathroom because you're embarrassed about what the other group members will think if you don't. There's a difference between baking cookies because you want to bless the people in your home and baking them because the last person who brought treats brought store-bought cookies and you think this will be more impressive.

I like how Peter approached this subject: "Above all, love each other deeply, because love covers over a multitude of sins. Offer hospitality to one another without grumbling. Each of you should use whatever gift you have received to serve others, as faithful stewards of God's grace in its various forms" (1 Peter 4:8–10).

So how do you as a group leader move away from task-oriented hospitality and toward a more biblical and robust hospitality? I'm still on that journey, but I think I've correctly identified the first step: repentance.

If you begrudge the tasks you have to perform in order to prepare for a group meeting—the money, time, and energy you spend week after week—then repent of your attitude and ask God to forgive you. Ask Him to make you more like Melchizedek, Rebekah, Abigail, and Jesus. Why? So you can offer yourself and your home as an act of love every time your group gets together.

Of course, prayer is a great way to make these requests of God. And prayer is also an important facet of hospitality.

The Role of Prayer in Hospitality

The kind of prayer I want to explore in this section is not "group prayer"—group members praying together during a gathering. Rather, the type of prayer connected to hospitality is a prayer of preparation the group leader or host prays outside of a gathering.

I'll soon offer some practical thoughts on how to carry out this method of prayer, but first I want to share some exciting research on the subject.

SURVEY TIME

Jim Egli served for years as small group pastor of the Vineyard Church in Urbana, Illinois. But he wasn't always confident in how to go about his role of equipping and supporting group leaders. Here's how Jim described his uncertainty:

> I kept hearing advice from a plethora of small-group authors and speakers, each promoting different methods and models. All of them were confident and persuasive, but their contradictory theories couldn't all be right. Someone needed to cut through the confusion by doing serious, scientific research on what really creates healthy, growing small groups. We needed to look past the models to discover the key underlying principles. I wanted to get to the bottom of things. I wanted an answer to the question, "What's the most important part of leading a small group?"[4]

So Jim did what anyone would do in that position: he completed a PhD in statistical analysis, teamed up with a research partner named Dwight Marable, and set out to conduct a comprehensive survey of three thousand group leaders in over two hundred churches across the country. (Okay, so Jim is probably the only person who would do that, but I'm glad he did.)

What Jim found was both surprising and exciting, to say the least. The survey literally contained hundreds of questions that probed into every detail of a person's role as a group leader. It covered group dynamics, leader behavior during group meetings, leader preparation before group meetings, leader qualifications (such as having a Bible degree), and more.

When the smoke cleared, the evidence was clear that one factor had more influence on the spiritual health of a small group than any other: the group leader's prayer life.

Egli's survey questions covered a wide range of tasks, behaviors, habits, and attitudes that could be adopted or practiced by group leaders. When he crunched the numbers, he saw right away that the following question had a high degree of correlation with a small group's spiritual health: "How much time do you spend on average praying for your small group meeting?"[5]

Along with that question, Egli found several other questions had a strong correlation with a group's spiritual health. These five, then, yielded the most pivotal results:

1. How consistently do you take time for prayer and Bible reading?
2. Are you praying daily for your non-Christian friends to come to know Jesus?
3. How many days in the past week did you pray for your small-group members?
4. Do you pray for your group meetings in the days leading up to it?[6]
5. How much time on average do you spend in daily prayer and Bible reading?

The results led Egli to this conclusion: "The leaders whose answers revealed a strong relationship with God had groups that were healthier and faster growing. These groups experienced a deeper level of care between members, had a clearer sense of mission beyond their group, and produced more leaders and new groups."[7]

In other words, group leaders with a strong prayer life were more likely to witness Spirit-driven growth not only in their own lives but in the lives of their group members.

In addition, group leaders demonstrating strong prayer lives witnessed greater evangelistic impact within their groups. Much greater, in fact. According to Egli and Marable's research, "Eighty-three percent of leaders with a strong prayer life reported that at least one person had come to Jesus through the influence of their group, while only 19 percent of leaders with a weak prayer life could say the same."[8]

OF VINES AND BRANCHES

When I first heard about the research conducted by these two men, I was skeptical. I wondered, *Could something as simple as prayer really have such a measurable impact on my small group week in and week out?* But the more I thought about it, the more I realized how silly that question was. Especially when you consider Jesus's words from John 15:4–8:

> Remain in me, as I also remain in you. No branch can bear fruit by itself; it must remain in the vine. Neither can you bear fruit unless you remain in me. I am the vine; you are the branches. If you remain in me and I in you, you will bear much fruit; apart from me you can do nothing. If you do not remain in me, you are like a branch that is thrown away and withers; such branches are picked up, thrown into the fire and burned. If you remain in me and my words remain in you, ask whatever you wish, and it will be done for you. This is to my Father's glory, that you bear much fruit, showing yourselves to be my disciples.

That's the key. When you pray for the members of your group and the corporate event of your group gathering, you plug into the Vine. You gain access to supernatural power. And, frankly, you get out of the Holy Spirit's way and let Him do the work He wants to do. This kind of prayer has everything to do with biblical hospitality because it involves giving your time and energy in an effort to bless others. Also, through this kind of prayer you're working to "make ready" the environment of your group meetings on a spiritual level.

I like the picture my friend Randall Neighbour paints of these twin levels of hospitality:

> There are two other very important things you must do before your small group members arrive: work on both the physical and spiritual climate of your home. Ensure that it's cool or warm enough in your home by adjusting your thermostat. Remember that your house will be filled with people, and the collective body heat will raise the thermometer within 20 minutes of the meeting's official starting time.
>
> To adjust the spiritual temperature of your home, take five minutes to sit in the room where you will meet and ask God to fill your home with His peace, leaving no room for anything evil such as strife or discord. Invite Him to come in power during the meeting. Sometimes, I will play praise music softly and pray for each member by name, asking God to touch him or her in a special way that night.[9]

Two climates: one physical, the other spiritual—and both key ingredients of biblical hospitality. Although given the research mentioned previously, your group will be better served if you spend more of your time preparing the spiritual climate through prayer.

Let's move on to some practical thoughts on how to carry out this kind of prayer.

PREPARATORY PRAYER

People pray and connect with God in many different ways, so I'm hesitant to set any kind of limits on or boundaries around how you approach this prayer of preparation. At the same time, I understand that having a few guidelines can be helpful in getting started. With that in mind, here are a few basic examples for how you can adjust the spiritual climate of your group meetings through prayer:

Pray for each of your group members every day. This is one of the most important steps you can take as a group leader. If your goal is to see group members experience spiritual growth, the best thing you can do is intercede for them with the Holy Spirit daily.

I recommend you pray for your group members as part of your regular devotional time. Pray that they will encounter God that day. Pray for their families. Pray for their jobs. Pray for whatever challenges they've identified within the group, and praise God for whatever victories and blessings they've experienced.

I also recommend that you pray for any group members you encounter throughout the course of your day. If you receive a text from someone in your group, for example, send up a quick word on their behalf: *Lord, please bless Sheila as she works today,* or *Father, thank You for leading Jerry to our group.*

Bracket your study times in prayer. Whenever you read over the curriculum your group is studying, start the process with prayer. Ask the Holy Spirit to give you wisdom and understanding as you explore the discussion questions or educational experiences you'll be leading the group into during your next meeting. Ask Him to spur the members of the group toward obedience and application.

When you're finished preparing for that group meeting,

pray again. Ask God to honor your efforts with spiritual fruit, to prepare the hearts of your group members, and to help you be effective as you attempt to lead.

Bracket each group meeting with prayer. Before the first person walks through your door, ask the Holy Spirit to be present as your group gathers. Specifically ask Him to remember the promise from Matthew 18:20: "Where two or three gather in my name, there am I with them." And after the last person leaves, pray again. Ask God to help you and your group members stay accountable when it comes to applying what you just learned.

These are just a few contexts for preparatory prayer I've found helpful in my journey as a small group leader. Be open-minded as you experiment with your own preferences and methods.

FINDING THE TIME TO PRAY

Right about now you may be thinking, *That sounds great, but I can't spend any more time preparing for group meetings than I already do. I'm maxed out.*

I hear you. I understand that because I've been maxed out myself. I remember more than a few times driving to a group meeting with my wife in the passenger seat frantically scribbling answers in our curriculum workbook. I also remember feeling frustrated when group members arrived early on our doorstep, because I still needed to vacuum the rugs and think up an icebreaker to start the discussion.

Fortunately, I've learned some tips and tricks over the years that help me free up time for the more important elements of hospitality—including prayer. Here are some examples:

Set reasonable expectations. When it comes to preparing the physical environment of our group meetings, I accomplish less than I used to. And I've learned that just because a lot of tasks and jobs are traditionally associated with leading a small group doesn't mean all those tasks and jobs are necessary. Or that I'm obligated to tackle them. Or that I'm obligated to tackle them as thoroughly as others might.

For example, I don't map out the discussion portion of our group meetings as meticulously as I used to. And my wife and I have toned down the pre-group cleanup around our house when we host. We make sure the bathroom is in good shape, of course, and we get dirty clothes and toys off the floor. But we're more willing to settle for "good enough" rather than work until everything is perfect. That means we give ourselves more time to pray.

Buy time when it's available and appropriate. If your group shares a meal together, for example, consider spending your money on a couple of pizzas rather than spending an afternoon's worth of time cooking up a Thanksgiving feast. Or download a prewritten Bible study every now and then rather than developing all your curriculum from scratch.

"Time is money" is a poor expression, but it's certainly true that money can buy some extra time for something as important as prayer.

Ask your group members for help. Many group leaders feel like they should be able to manage whatever is necessary to keep the group running smoothly. Whether they want to be in control or they don't want to admit something that could be perceived as failure, they basically hog all the ministry responsibilities within the group. But that's not healthy for the group leader or the group members. Because when participants take on additional responsibilities within the group, their level of commitment to the group rises.

So be honest with your group members. Talk to them about all the different tasks and responsibilities you think are necessary to keep the group running smoothly. Be honest with them about the amount of time you have available and the tasks you're willing to fulfill. And then ask for help with everything else.

The Necessary Element of Fun

I've covered two facets of hospitality so far in this chapter:

> ➤ Performing chores in preparation for a group meeting can be beneficial, provided you do so out of a desire to bless others.
> ➤ Committing to regular prayer in preparation for a group meeting will help create a spiritual climate conducive to spiritual growth.

Now it's time for the third facet: fun. And here's my summary statement to go along with the other two: *including the element of fun in your group meetings will help create an atmosphere that blesses others and leads to spiritual growth.*

That's right! It's my belief that fun is a necessary facet of small group hospitality because it supplements and supports the other two facets.

Fun is crucial to a small group meeting for two reasons, and everybody understands the first one. Namely, it's fun to have fun. People like having fun. You, me, your group members, and anyone who might eventually become one of your group members—we all enjoy a good time.

People feel blessed when they have fun, and having fun in a group setting creates positive associations. It helps people open up and speeds up the process of building relationships. At the very least, it gives people a concrete reason to come back even if other parts of the group meeting don't go very well. (Of course, the opposite is true for boring or overly serious group meetings.)

The second reason having fun is important for groups is a bit more surprising. Namely, fun is a key component of spiritual growth. Think about it. How many feasts did God command the Israelites to celebrate throughout the Old Testament? (Not "recommend," by the way, but "command.") How many parties did Jesus and His disciples attend? How many times does the Bible record members of the early church breaking bread together?

But my favorite example of this principle comes from Nehemiah 8. The Israelites had finished rebuilding the wall around Jerusalem in record time, and Nehemiah gathered them for a kind of festival of dedication. A teacher of the law named Ezra read aloud from the law of Moses "from daybreak till noon" (Neh. 8:3). While he read, other Levites circulated among the crowds, "making it clear and giving the meaning so that the people understood what was being read" (v. 8).

What happened next was natural: the people wept. They'd evidently not been exposed to the law for a long time and had drifted into sin yet again. So they mourned.

But not for long:

> Then Nehemiah the governor, Ezra the priest and teacher of the Law, and the Levites who were instructing the people said to them all, "This day is holy to the LORD your God. Do not mourn or weep." For all the people had been weeping as they listened to the words of the Law.
>
> Nehemiah said, "Go and enjoy choice food and sweet drinks, and send some to those who have nothing prepared. This day is holy to our Lord. Do not grieve, for the joy of the LORD is your strength."
>
> The Levites calmed all the people, saying, "Be still, for this is a holy day. Do not grieve."
>
> Then all the people went away to eat and drink, to send portions of food and to celebrate with great joy, because they now understood the words that had been made known to them. (Neh. 8:9–12)

As a groups guy, I love everything about that passage. You have people gathering together. They're exposed to the truth through God's Word. They're interacting with that truth, discussing it and learning new information. And the Holy Spirit moves as a result, causing conviction of sin and ultimately spiritual growth.

That's a great picture of the kind of group meeting I'm advocating in this book! And the entire event is underscored and uplifted by the element of fun.

So what does it take to make fun a key cog in your small groups machine? Each group will have its own preferences, of course, but there are a couple of items I feel comfortable recommending. I've separated them out based on the essential activities of a group meeting I highlighted in chapter 1.

Social connection and fellowship. Social connection is all about fun, of course, but a lot of times this is an unofficial portion of a group meeting—it's understood that people will "hang out" until everyone is gathered and the meeting begins.

I, however, recommend making social connection an "officially sanctioned" portion of each group meeting. Make it known that you want your group members to spend time enjoying each other's company. And be sure to set a good example by joining in the fellowship yourself.

What about timing? Some groups like to be social at the beginning of a meeting; others like to save the fellowship until the end. I say, why not have both? This is just my opinion, but I think an ideal setup is fifteen to twenty minutes of social interaction at the beginning of the gathering. Then have an official time when the group meeting ends, but make it known that everyone is welcome to stay and hang out for as long as they'd like (or as long as is reasonable for the hosts).

Interaction with God's Word. The Bible is not a boring book, and it has a lot to say on subjects like joy and humor. Think of David's exuberant expressions throughout the psalms, for example. Or the absurd hilarity of Jesus's story about a man with a log in his eye trying to pull a speck from the eye of someone else. Those passages are fun, and so are many others. So emphasize them in the course of your study.

Group discussion. Not all discussion questions have to be somber or deep. You can ask questions that are creative and off-the-wall. Even silly. I think this is especially helpful as a way to approach Scripture passages or topics that are confusing or complex. For example, say, "I'll give a dollar to anyone who can name all the materials used to build the statue in Nebuchadnezzar's dream. Any takers?"

Learning activities. Learning activities provide an outlet for physical movement, creativity, artistic expression, and competition. As such, they're fertile soil for fun. (We'll explore these activities more thoroughly in Part Two.)

Prayer. Praise and thanksgiving are important elements of prayer, and they can both be fun if you make an effort in that direction. For example, consider giving the group a chance to "shout for joy" as part of your prayer time.

Worship. Worship can be solemn and silent at times, but it can also be "a joyful noise." Or what if you asked your group members to follow David's example of "leaping and dancing before the LORD" (2 Sam. 6:16). How fun would that be?

Application. Sometimes it's tough to obey what you've learned from God's Word, and other times obedience requires sacrifice. But often it's exhilarating to see God work in your life as you obey Him. Plus, the reason "doing good is its own reward" is that doing good is fun—especially when you do good with a group of people you enjoy spending time with.

My point in creating this list is not to make you feel like you have to artificially inject something hilarious into every section of every group meeting. (That wouldn't be fun to plan, for one thing.) No, my point is that you don't have to compartmentalize fun into the beginning or end of your gatherings. You don't have to say, "We'll have some fun, and then we'll discuss the text, pray, sing some songs— and then we'll have fun again."

Rather, by offering a few opportunities for participants to have fun throughout your group meetings, you'll bless them with a good time, and you'll take another step toward maintaining an atmosphere conducive to spiritual growth.

Chapter 4

Are Small Groups Still Relevant?

It was a cloudy Sunday morning in March at Gateway Fellowship Church near San Antonio, Texas. The usual parking attendants went about their usual work in their usual yellow vests. The usual collection of family cars and trucks (a lot of trucks, since it was Texas) made their way through the parking lot and arranged themselves in their usual lines at the typical time.

But that's where the "usual" ended. Because this was March of 2020, smack in the middle of the COVID-19 pandemic. Which is why none of the churchgoers got out of their cars. They all stayed in their seats, kids included, and tuned their radios to 94.7 FM so they could hear what was going on.

You see, this was Gateway's first drive-in church service. This was their first attempt at "doing church" in the midst of the lockdowns and prohibitions on gatherings set in place throughout most of the state.

To their credit, the folks at Gateway went all out. The worship band assembled on the church roof and played their hearts out. The pastor preached overlooking a sea of cars. The church's social media director even designed a "drive-in worship guide" to help church-goers participate and feel included in this new form of church service. That guide offered the following car-based cues:

> - **Parking lights on:** "I am ready to worship."
> - **Headlights on:** "I am singing along."
> - **Right turn signal:** "Raising one hand in worship."
> - **Wipers on:** "Lifting both hands in worship."
> - **Flash brights:** "Amen! Preach it!"
> - **Left turn signal:** "I want to turn from my sins."
> - **Hazard lights:** "I am in need of prayer."
> - **Spray washer fluid:** "I wanna be baptized!"[1]

I'm sure you have stories about learning to navigate a new way of life because of COVID-19. The pandemic had a major impact on so many of our usual rituals and routines: our work and careers, our social lives, our sports, our approaches to medicine, our attendance at church—and yes, our small groups.

But COVID-19 hasn't been the only disruptor of our group experiences across recent years. The internet has been changing the world in drastic ways for decades now. And as new technology continues to develop faster speeds and manage larger amounts of data, the internet is impacting many of the factors that draw people to groups and groups ministry in the first place, such as community, fellowship, education, worship, prayer, and even relational depth.

All of this raises the question *Are small groups still relevant?* Does community-based ministry still have a place in a world where people continue to fear face-to-face interaction? Do physical gatherings make sense in a culture that's moving more and more online?

I firmly believe the answer to those questions is yes. In fact, I firmly believe that small groups and groups-based ministries are *more* relevant today than at any point in my lifetime. To show you why, let's start with a little history.

A Quick History of Small Groups

One of the questions people often ask is, "When did small groups start?" As in, when did small groups become a thing in the church? When did they start getting popular?

The easy answer is that small groups have been part of the church for as long as there's been a church. In fact, as I mentioned in chapter 2, small groups *were* the church during its earliest foundations. The members of the early church, both in Jerusalem and in gentile cities, primarily met in homes—especially after Christians began to be barred from the temple and local synagogues.

Not until Roman emperor Constantine officially embraced Christianity were followers of Jesus able to gather freely in public. That freedom led to the construction of cathedrals and other gathering places, which eventually moved "church" from houses to separate buildings.

In the centuries that followed, Catholicism continued to expand across modern-day Europe, Africa, and Asia. Always well organized, the church functioned as an interconnected web of parish networks. These parish congregations functioned similarly to how the house churches of the earliest Christians operated, with the notable exception of centralized church buildings. In many cases, those parish chapels and cathedrals were the hub of both spiritual and social life within villages and regions. People "did life together" as a church, and the community connection of those parishes was strong.

In other areas, people began to cluster in more isolated communities, like monasteries, convents, and religious orders. Typically, members of these communities agreed to live by a specific set of expectations or instructions, which were called "rules." Once again, the overall goal of such clusters was to collectively experience spiritual growth. The process for that growth mirrored many elements we associate with groups today: accountability, discussion, worship, prayer, and service.

Jumping forward a bit, small groups played a big role in the Protestant Reformation of the sixteenth century and beyond. The reformers, including Martin Luther and John Calvin, were firm advocates for "the priesthood of believers," the idea that Scripture was not reserved for priests but should be accessed and explored by all disciples of Jesus. That emphasis led to many smaller gatherings of followers with the purpose of studying God's Word and talking through ways to apply Scripture to everyday life.

John Wesley was another reformer who emphasized small groups and revolutionized the church in England and America. So-called class meetings were at the heart of his Methodist movement, in which people gathered weekly (at a minimum) to study Scripture, read helpful books, and partake of Communion. Participation in a group was required for membership in the Methodist church, and that participation went a long way toward helping believers practice what they encountered in God's Word.

The Puritans used a similar approach across Europe and into America. One important element in that culture was gathering in "private meetings," which were designed to help members grow spiritually through prayer, understand the Bible, serve, learn how to express their faith, and more.[2]

Other important historical figures include Philipp Jakob Spener in the Pietist movement, the Moravians, the cell church movement, and the modern renewal of house churches.

Another big moment in small groups history was the advent of Sunday schools. Here's a little-known fact: the Sunday school movement got started before the public school movement. A man named Robert Raikes in Gloucester, England, noticed that large numbers of children were running unsupervised on Sundays—their only day off from working in mills and factories. Many of those children were orphans.

Raikes organized Sunday schools as a way of connecting with and caring for those children, as well as giving them an education to help change the trajectories of their futures. And it worked! Sunday schools became a huge phenomenon in England and into America, where they eventually morphed into the model we associate with Sunday school in churches today.

More recently, what we often think of as small group ministry began to take shape in America in the 1970s and '80s. Pioneers including Lyman Coleman and Ralph Neighbour cut their teeth in the twelve-step movement and the house-church movement, respectively. Both launched publishing houses and training networks to help leaders launch and maintain their groups, which were often "underground" and unsupported by local churches. Other organizations like the Navigators used small groups as a key tool for evangelism.

Those ministries continued to evolve in the '80s and '90s when they became more integrated into "regular" church life. They have continued to grow in popularity in the twenty-first century—although it's yet to be determined what role groups will have in the church in a post-COVID world.

What's my point with this little history lesson? Simply to show you that groups have always been part of the church, and I believe they will always be part of the church on this side of eternity. Groups-centered approaches to ministry have been adapting to changes in culture for two thousand years now, and they will continue to adapt and support the church's overall mission.

Also, I want you to see that leading a group means you're part of a long and noble tradition. You're joining and extending the work begun by those earliest apostles—Peter and Paul and James and Priscilla and more. You're joining a movement that's spanned centuries and denominations.

Yes, it may be true that what we think of as "groups" are changing and adapting once more, but that's good. That's healthy and productive. And now you have the opportunity to add your voice and your experiences to this increasingly fruitful movement.

Groups Are Good for the Culture

Something strange has been happening in our world over the past decade or so. Okay, lots of strange things have been happening, but I'm thinking of one thing in particular. The phenomenon I have in mind is a bit hard to articulate, but I think it can be expressed in two seemingly contradictory statements.

First, people in our world are more connected than they've ever been. This is true for lots of reasons, but they mostly boil down to technology. The internet has made the globe smaller. Cell phones have made it possible to speak with anyone in the world easily and inexpensively. Social media has opened the door for limitless connections between people over limitless issues and topics.

I haven't spoken with my old college roommate for twenty years. But if I wanted to know what he ate for breakfast this morning, I could probably find out. That's how connected our world has become.

Here's the second statement: people in our world are more lonely than they've ever been. Again, there's lots of evidence to support that claim. A recent survey revealed that 61 percent of Americans would describe themselves as lonely. Digging deeper into the results, the survey showed that 73 percent of "very heavy" social media users were lonely. Strangely, it was the younger generations (Gen Z and Millennials) who scored highest in terms of their overall loneliness, rather than older generations.[3]

Loneliness has become so bad, in fact, that the United Kingdom appointed a Minister for Loneliness as a key government official. In announcing that position, the British Prime Minister said, "For far too many people, loneliness is the sad reality of modern life."[4] And that was before COVID-19.

How can we reconcile those two truths? The world is more connected than ever before, and yet people are more lonely than ever before. What do those realities tell us about ourselves?

For me, they tell us that human beings aren't wired merely for connection. We need community. We need deep and meaningful relationships.

That's bad news for our culture today. We've spent years doing everything possible to build a world of unlimited connections, to link ourselves together both literally and metaphorically. Despite all our efforts, it hasn't worked. People are lonely. People are isolated. People are anxious. People are afraid.

This is good news for the church. Why? Because the church can offer what our culture is missing: community. Real relationships. Meaningful conversation. Important and necessary work within local cities and neighborhoods. The church can offer a picture of the abundant life Jesus promised in Scripture (see John 10:10).

This is especially true of small groups. Because groups are built on the foundation of community.

The more people feel dissatisfied with surface-level interactions on social media, the more small groups can offer meaningful engagement. The more people become frustrated with fleeting connections online, the more small groups can offer relationships that last. And the more people become afraid of being canceled or ostracized because of stray opinions (past or present), the more small groups can offer acceptance, love, and hope.

So yes, small groups are still relevant in a virtual world. In fact, in many ways, groups are the antidote to our online addiction.

Groups Are Good for the Church

We just explored something strange that's been happening in our culture, so it's only fair that I mention something strange happening with the church in recent years: it's shrinking. And it's shrinking in more ways than one.

The obvious way is the decline in overall church attendance, which I mentioned in chapter 2. Fewer and fewer people are deciding to visit churches (or synagogues or mosques), attend services, and become members. Worse, that trend is accelerating. Only 47 percent of American adults said they were members of any religious organization (again, church, synagogue, or mosque) in 2020, down from about 70 percent in 1999.[5]

What might be most alarming is that this downward trend is especially pronounced among younger generations. In 2019 (which means before COVID), roughly two-thirds of Millennials attended worship services only "a few times a year" or less. Forty percent of Millennials said they never or seldom went to church.[6] In recent years, between 50 and 88 percent of Gen-Z students who did attend church growing up stopped attending after their first year of college.[7]

So yes, the church is shrinking in terms of attendance. But it's also shrinking in terms of its overall influence in communities.

One reason for that loss of influence is the number of churches that closed their doors during the COVID-19 pandemic but never opened them back up. Many churches were forced to shutter for good. Beyond that, the churches that have been successful have been *really* successful. I'm talking about megachurches, which have grown over the past decade and had the fiscal and technological resources to adapt to COVID-19 and survive—sometimes even thrive.

In short, there are fewer churches in our culture than there used to be. Which means there are fewer touch points in a given community for people to encounter and engage with the truth of God's Word and followers of Christ.

Once again, groups can help.

That's because groups ministries are an excellent touch point for the church in every community. They're easy to launch, easy to adjust, easy to grow, and easy to multiply. They're flexible rather than static. They're personal rather than imposing. And they're relational rather than superficial.

Just about any place you typically spend time can serve as a location for a small group. That includes your workplace, your local community center, your favorite restaurant, your regular gym, and your local bookshop. Small groups can thrive in your home, in prisons, in hospitals, in conference rooms, in parks, and just about any other place people tend to gather.

And yes, groups can thrive in church buildings.

In short, small groups are an effective liaison between our culture and a church in decline. Which, in my book, makes them relevant.

What about Small Groups 2.0?

I mentioned earlier that the concept of small groups and small groups ministry has been undergoing some changes in recent years. One of the biggest changes is the increasing acceptance and use of online platforms to conduct group gatherings.

These are Zoom groups. Or virtual groups. Or whatever other name people use to describe communities that meet regularly through the internet rather than gathering in the same physical location.

Of course, the prevalence of online groups has skyrocketed since the COVID-19 pandemic made it preferable to avoid being in the same physical location as others—at least for a time.

Clearly, online groups have some real advantages, even in comparison with "regular" group gatherings. For example, online groups allow you to meet with people not physically located in your community. You can host people from several different states, or even several different countries, as long as everyone gets the time zones worked out correctly.

Online groups also offer a lot of flexibility in terms of meeting times and schedules. They don't require people to commute, which saves time. They don't require childcare to be arranged. And they allow people to connect at pretty much any time of day as long as they have a phone and a working Wi-Fi connection.

And yes, online groups can offer a higher level of comfort than in-person groups can, especially during those first few meetings. You don't have to walk into someone else's home. Instead, you can log on from the comfort of your favorite chair, even wearing your favorite sweats if you want.

Some weaknesses are associated with online groups as well. The worst, in my opinion, is the unpredictability of technology. Video connections aren't always reliable, and it can be quite irritating when one or more group members lag. We've all been on those video conferences where someone's mouth starts moving but you don't hear anything for a second or two. "I think what Paul was communicating is— Oh, can you hear me?"

Also, non-talking elements in an online group gathering can present some real limitations. Like worship, for example. Playing a few songs over my portable speakers is a lot different from joining my voice with others in the same room. (These deficiencies make sense, given that our best video-conferencing technologies so far were designed primarily to facilitate meetings between work colleagues.)

And as we'll see in later chapters, lots of nonverbal communication typically happens in a group setting. Physical postures. Leaning in or leaning away. Eye contact. These are important elements of group interaction, and they're important cues for group leaders when it comes to what group members appreciate and what they need. Those cues can be lost when the leader is trying to follow fourteen separate video feeds.

I want to communicate one more thing about online groups, but I'll preface it by saying this is merely my opinion. Remember when Paul was talking about marriage in 1 Corinthians 7, and he started prefacing his comments? "To the rest I say this (I, not the Lord)" (v. 12). Well, I want to use that some pattern here.

My final thought about online groups is from Sam, not the Lord. And that opinion is this: online groups have a place, but they fall short of what in-person groups can offer.

Specifically, I think online groups fall short of the community and relational depth that can be achieved through in-person groups. Something about being physically present with others facilitates genuine connection and community. Something about breaking bread with others establishes bonds. And something about laying hands on each other in prayer—or even that quick, silly side hug at the beginning of a gathering—communicates in a way that goes far beyond speaking.

I believe that's what our culture is missing today—physical connection. Side-by-side interaction. Genuine community. And in my mind, that opportunity for community is what makes small groups more relevant and more important than ever.

Chapter 5

Learning Styles

Just before Christmas one year, my son Daniel told me about a scene from one of his favorite Thomas the Tank Engine videos. "Diesel was chuffing away from Thomas," he said, "but Thomas was trying to catch him and stop him from being naughty." As he spoke, Daniel started waving his hands back and forth in front of his face, and then he clapped them together at the word *naughty*.

"Diesel went around a big curve on the mountain. He was racing very fast, and Thomas was racing very fast too." Now Daniel was rocking back and forth on his legs, and his hands were still clapping and rubbing together in front of his chest. "Then the track was missing in front of Diesel because the bridge wasn't finished yet! Diesel tried to stop and *squeeeaaaked* with his brakes." My son pistoned his legs up and down, stretching out the word *squeaked* in a good example of onomatopoeia.

I could tell the tension in Daniel's story was rising because he literally started running around in circles as he continued to talk. "Diesel went right to the edge, and he almost fell into the river. But he stopped. But he was hanging off the track and couldn't get back on." Daniel had finished the little circles, but now his hips were wiggling back and forth, and he was chafing his fingers together like a doctor washing his hands before surgery. "Thomas came behind Diesel and coupled up to him. Then Thomas pulled Diesel away from the hole in the tracks! Thomas was the hero, and he saved Diesel!"

This was the climax of the story, and Daniel sprinted away from my seat on the couch, made a circle around the dining room table, sprinted back, and then collapsed next to me, breathing hard.

If someone outside of our home had seen Daniel tell his story, that person might have said my son had "ants in his pants" or had been eating too much sugar. They may have even tried to get Daniel to stand still or sit down.

But I knew my son's wiggling and jiggling were perfectly normal. It's just one of the ways he demonstrates a strong tendency toward a kinesthetic (or physical) learning style. Meaning, whenever his brain is busy processing a lot of information (whether coming in or going out), his arms and legs want to shake and quake. For him, the process of thinking is connected to movement, which is common for young boys.

As Daniel's father, it's important that I know my son well enough to understand his learning styles so I can use them to my advantage when I try to communicate with him—especially if I want to help him explore something important or complex. Otherwise I would be in danger of forming misconceptions about what he needs and is capable of.

Learning styles are also an important tool for leading transformational group meetings, and I want to explore that connection as we move through this chapter.

A Brief Overview of Learning Styles

Here's a quick definition of learning styles to get us started: *a learning style refers to how a person perceives and processes information.*

To *perceive* information refers to the way a person takes in or receives data from the outside world. So we can receive data through our eyes, our ears, our nose, our fingers. To *process* information refers to what a person's brain does with all that data after it's been perceived—how the data is interpreted, categorized, stored, and used.

As a group leader, it's important that you understand how learning styles work and influence your efforts at preparing for and leading group gatherings.

First, you need to understand the different types of learning styles the members of your group might demonstrate. This will be vital information as you prepare to lead the essential activities for each group meeting (fellowship, interaction with God's Word, group discussion, learning activities, prayer, worship, and application). Ideally, you'll get to the point where you know the specific learning styles of each person in your group so you can tailor those essential activities to fit those preferences.

Second, you need to understand how *you* perceive and process information. Understanding your own learning style will help you get the most out of each group meeting. It will also keep you from attempting to lead others only through the lens of your own learning style (more on that later).

The VARK Model

If you're interested in research, you might like to know that several different approaches categorize and label learning styles. Some of them are scholarly, some are kind of silly, and a few make sense and are easy to understand. I prefer the latter.[1] And that's why I'll be focusing on the VARK model developed by the late Neil Fleming. It's a little more approachable than some of the other models out there—and it works well for me.[2]

The VARK model identifies four distinct learning styles:

> **Visual:** learning best through seeing
> **Aural:** learning best through hearing
> **Read/Write:** learning best through words on a page
> **Kinesthetic:** learning best through experience and touch

Maybe you're thinking, *Hey, I can do all those things! I can see, hear, read, write, and touch.* And that's true. But the idea behind learning styles is that you and I have preferences when it comes to how we perceive and process information. We tend to drift more strongly toward a certain learning style—referred to as our dominant style—as we interact with the world. Many people also have a secondary style they're comfortable with in learning as well.

The next four sections of this chapter dig deeper into all four of the VARK learning styles, including the major characteristics of each style, how those characteristics manifest themselves in everyday life, and how they can be applied to a group setting.

But first I want to tackle the question *Why?*

Why Learning Styles?

Group leaders need to have a proper understanding of learning styles for three important reasons.

1. **Learning styles influence how group members learn.** I know that sounds obvious—to say that learning styles have an impact on how people learn. But it's a significant idea for both you and the other members of your group. Put simply, when your group members have a proper understanding of how they learn best, they will learn more. They'll be better equipped to engage whatever curriculum you're studying, and they'll be better equipped to interact with and understand each other.

2. **Learning styles influence how group leaders lead.** Your

dominant learning style has a major influence on how you, as a group leader, perceive and process information from the world. But your dominant learning style has just as much influence on how you *present* that information to other people. Meaning, we tend to teach and lead others based on the way we prefer to learn.

Small group leaders who are dominant in the reading/ writing learning style often structure group meetings around activities associated with reading and writing—making assignments in a workbook, for example, or reading contextual information out loud. Doing so may unintentionally ignore the needs and preferences of others in the group who learn visually, aurally, or kinesthetically. (The same is true of group leaders with the other dominant learning styles.)

3. **Learning styles influence the interpersonal dynamics of the group.** When people have a hard time forming a relationship because their personalities don't mix well, we refer to that as a "personality clash." A similar phenomenon can happen with learning styles—especially in a group setting where ideas are regularly explained, discussed, processed, and applied. Group members can become frustrated when others approach these tasks in different and sometimes competing ways.

I'm a read/write learner, for example, and I can remember feeling exasperated when people in one of my earlier groups kept rehashing the meaning of certain doctrines through an extended conversation. I would think, *Why don't they just read the definition written right there in the workbook?* Now I understand those individuals were auditory learners, and they wanted to process those definitions through conversation.

Conversely, the reality of learning styles also presents

group members with the chance to demonstrate love to each other. When we're patient with others who learn differently—and especially when we make an effort to engage others in their preferred learning styles—we're loving them as ourselves.

A quick side note: In chapter 1, I made it clear that learning information should not be the primary purpose of a group meeting. But I want to emphasize that the process of learning—of perceiving and processing information—is an important part of any group meeting. Learning is an important part of spiritual growth, which is the primary purpose of a group meeting.

For one thing, the act of learning permeates all the essential activities that make up an effective group gathering. Obviously, learning plays a big part in group discussions and interactions with the Bible. But group members also learn about each other when they engage in fellowship and share pieces of their stories through prayer. And group members learn more about God when they study the Bible, work to apply what it says, and worship Him.

For another thing, the act of learning puts us in contact with the Holy Spirit. Here's how Jesus introduced the Spirit to the earliest leaders of the church: "The Advocate, the Holy Spirit, whom the Father will send in my name, will *teach* you all things and will remind you of everything I have said to you" (John 14:26, emphasis added).

Not only does the Spirit teach us, but as we gain new information and ideas, we give the Spirit more surface area to bring about change in our lives. As I gain understanding about the doctrines of sin and temptation, for example, I give the Holy Spirit opportunities to push me toward conviction and repentance. When I learn about the unique attributes of God, the Spirit can use that knowledge to nudge me toward greater experiences of worship and praise.

In short, under the direction of the Holy Spirit, acquiring

information is an important step in the process of transformation. And that's another reason you as a group leader should be aware of the following learning styles.

Visual Learners

People with a visual learning style prefer to perceive information through their eyes. They like it when facts and ideas are organized visually into charts, graphs, diagrams, and maps. They often communicate their thoughts through similes and metaphors that rely on images—"I was as nervous as a long-tailed cat in a room full of rocking chairs."

Visual learners are also good at spatial recognition. They're aware of their physical surroundings and are able to visualize the layout of rooms and buildings. They're skilled at working with shapes and objects, even to the point of rotating and manipulating them in their mind's eye.

Visual learners often enjoy expressing themselves artistically through drawing, painting, sculpting, and so forth. If they're forced to sit and listen to a lecture or take notes, you may catch them doodling shapes and patterns on their paper as a kind of "visual venting."

Here are some other cues and clues that may help you recognize a visual learner:

> ➤ If you asked a visual learner for directions, he would probably draw you a map.
> ➤ When a visual learner orders food at a restaurant, she looks at the pictures on a menu or at meals being eaten at the other tables.
> ➤ Visual learners gravitate toward books with color illustrations and complicated diagrams.
> ➤ Documents and presentations put together by a visual learner will use a wide variety of fonts, colors, images, and graphs.

> A Bible owned by a visual learner may be highlighted in different colors as a method of taking notes.
> Visual learners often use words and phrases like these: *vision*, *view*, *I'm trying to visualize*, *see the point*, and *draw up*.

VISUAL LEARNERS IN SMALL GROUPS

Unfortunately, much of the "traditional" small group experience doesn't appeal to visual learners. For one thing, few Bible studies and curriculum guides contain helpful charts, graphs, or diagrams. And group leaders often don't think to produce any kind of visual aids to supplement these materials. Many curriculum guides provide space for group members to "fill in the blank" as a method of taking notes or recording their thoughts, whereas visual learners would prefer to draw a picture or set up a chart.

In addition, most small groups are based on talking. We talk to each other during fellowship time. We discuss the Bible and what it means during study time. We verbalize our prayer requests and sing songs during worship time. While visual learners aren't usually opposed to talking, they would be more stimulated and probably retain more of what they hear if groups included a wider variety of activities.

Here are some ways you as a group leader can make visual learners more comfortable and more engaged:

Find visual aids. Try to find visual aids that supplement whatever curriculum or Bible study your group is following. And if you can't find any, consider producing your own charts, graphs, diagrams—anything that puts a visual structure to facts and ideas. Or have your visual learners produce their own chart or diagram during the group meeting.

Use props and object lessons. Including physical objects and demonstrations in a group meeting is another way to engage visual learners. If you're discussing how Christ is the light of the world, for example, illustrate the idea by lighting a candle in a dark room. Or set up a cross for visual learners to focus on during prayer.

Have a craft time. Visual learners enjoy expressing themselves artistically, so add an "arts and crafts" element to your group every now and then. Bring in crayons and colored pencils and ask the group to draw something, or bring in Play-Doh and have them sculpt something. Of course, it won't help to have them create something random—make sure it's connected to the topic of discussion.

Use multimedia. See if you can identify a movie clip or video that would effectively illustrate the concept or idea your group will be discussing. Or have a visual group member search for one on their phone during the discussion.

Emphasize the visual in Scripture. Many portions of the Bible are visual—especially the psalms, the prophets, and apocalyptic texts such as Revelation. When you notice a text that's heavy on visual elements, be sure to call them out. Make the visual nature of the verses a large part of the discussion.

Aural (or Auditory) Learners

Aural is the VARK label, but let's use *auditory*.

People with an auditory learning style prefer to perceive information through their ears, and they often use their mouths to process that information. They like concepts and ideas explained to them, and they like to explain concepts and ideas to others. That's why they're big fans of lectures, both giving and receiving them. They may also be gifted at public speaking.

Auditory learners thrive in discussion-based environments. They benefit from talking through what they've learned and what they're feeling, and they're generally good at listening to others. They also enjoy participating in and listening to debates.

Many auditory learners demonstrate a strong connection to music and sounds. They often have a good sense of rhythm and enjoy singing and playing an instrument.

Here are some other cues and clues that may help you recognize an auditory learner:

> If you ask an auditory learner for directions, she might explain which roads you should take and which landmarks to watch for in detail.
> When an auditory learner orders food at a restaurant, he listens carefully when the server talks about the specials. He may also ask questions about items on the menu.
> Auditory learners enjoy audio books. And if they're reading a hardcopy book, they'll probably turn on some music in the background.
> Cell phones were a perfect invention for auditory learners because they allow people to talk at almost any time and in almost any place.
> If an auditory learner is watching a live sports event, she may try to engage others around her in a conversation about what's happening on the field or court.
> Auditory learners often use words and phrases like these: *I hear you, that sounds right, listen to me,* and *let me explain.*

AUDITORY LEARNERS IN SMALL GROUPS

As you can see from the characteristics just described, small groups are an ideal setting for auditory learners. Whereas the traditional emphasis on talking in small groups is a negative for visual learners, it creates a positive atmosphere for auditory learners. For that reason, auditory learners gravitate naturally toward groups, and they probably make up a large percentage of your group.

Here's how you can make sure those auditory learners benefit from your group experience:

Discuss, discuss, discuss. Most small groups are based on discussion, which is a big reason they continue to grow in popularity. Continue giving your people chances to both talk and listen.

Read Scripture out loud. For some people, reading a Bible passage out loud is a terrifying experience. But that's usually not the case for auditory learners. So when your group is exploring a specific passage of Scripture, ask for volunteers to read the text out loud at least one time during the group meeting.

Pray out loud. The same idea applies here. Encourage group members to pray out loud if they would like to do so.

Sing and make music. In an earlier chapter, I've already mentioned that group leaders shouldn't limit themselves to singing as an expression of worship. But that doesn't mean they should eliminate singing, either. Give your group members a chance to verbally express their devotion to God through songs, responsive readings, and spontaneous prayer.

Let me say one more thing about auditory learners: don't be too quick about labeling someone in your group as a person who "talks too much." That every group contains at least one person who feels a need to answer every question or dominate each conversation is a common idea in group ministry. But it's often a misconception.

I had to grapple with this issue when "Mary" and her husband joined our young couples group.[3] Mary was a talker, plain and simple. Energetic and extroverted, she was the life of the party at every gathering, and she enthusiastically jumped into our discussions with an eagerness to learn that was refreshing to see.

She had this one habit, though. Whenever the group finished discussing a topic and started moving toward something else, she would stop everything in order to jump in and summarize what we had just talked about, like this: "Okay, so we're saying that when Jesus talks about the kingdom of God, He's talking about our time here on earth but also about a time in the future with the new heaven and new earth. That's what you mean by 'already and not yet.'"

That habit annoyed me. I felt like Mary was trying to get in the last word on each issue we discussed. I felt like she was showing off. I even felt like she was usurping my role as the group leader a little bit. And because of all that, I considered confronting her about it—all in the name of improving our group experience, of course.

Fortunately, I talked this through with my wife before I took any action. "She's not doing anything wrong," Jess told me. "She's just making sure she understands, and talking about it out loud probably helps her keep her thoughts straight."

We didn't know it at the time, but Jess was correctly identifying Mary as an auditory learner. Mary's habit of summing up the main ideas of our discussion was in no way malicious or self-seeking; it was a learning tool. Speaking the ideas out loud helped her process the information she heard during our discussion, just like I processed the same information by taking notes.

Not everyone is like Mary, however. Some people legitimately "talk too much," dominating discussions and other activities within a group meeting. And others are socially unaware to the point that they don't realize other people in the group have grown uncomfortable with their over-talking. (I'll give some guidance on helping these people in chapter 13.)

But before you label anyone "too talkative"—and definitely before you approach them in an effort to have them talk less—take a step back and make sure you're evaluating the situation correctly. Is that person's behavior really causing damage to your group? Or are they simply operating normally in their preferred style of learning?

Read/Write Learners

People with a read/write learning style choose to perceive and process information by, well, reading and writing. If they're assigned to learn something, they go straight to a book and research the given topic. If they're asked to explain a concept or idea to another person, they summarize what they've read about that concept or idea. And when they listen to a lecture or sermon, they process that auditory experience by writing copious notes.

Read/write learners even turn to books as a means of artistic enjoyment and expression. They enjoy literature and good prose, and they often collect vast libraries (when they can afford it). They can write both creatively and practically, moving from a grocery list to poetry without any need to change gears.

Here are some cues and clues that may help you recognize a read/write learner:

> If you ask a read/write learner for directions, he'll jot down the appropriate streets and turns in list form.
> When a read/write learner orders food at a restaurant, she's read the menu or consulted the restaurant's website beforehand to decide what she wants.
> Read/write learners place a high value on well-written quotations and clever word games.
> Read/write learners place a high value on published authors, often desiring to write their own books one day.
> People who spend a lot of time making to-do lists are often read/write learners.
> A read/write learner would rather email you or text message you than call your phone directly.
> Read/write learners often use phrases like these: *Can you text that to me? I just read about this! I need to write that down.*

READ/WRITE LEARNERS IN GROUPS

As with auditory learners, small groups present advantages to people with a read/write learning style. The idea of a Bible study or curriculum guide is exciting for them, as is the opportunity to study the Bible directly. These individuals also enjoy the traditional "inductive Bible study" format, where they're asked to read a portion of the text, interpret what it means, and then make a connection toward application.

Read/write learners usually enjoy group discussions—especially when they're given the opportunity to recite definitions, make connections to other parts of Scripture, and dig into the study notes in their Bibles.

Here are more methods to maximize a group experience for read/write learners:

Allow for homework. I know, I know. For a lot of people, *homework* is a dirty word. But not for read/write learners. They don't like making spontaneous judgments about a text and prefer to study, take notes, and answer questions during the week in order to be fully prepared for the group discussion.

So don't totally abandon the idea of homework, but don't make it mandatory for all your group members, either. Make it an option.

Include reading time. If your small group is approaching a Bible passage or a book for the first time, be sure to provide a few minutes for people to read it over more than once. Give your read/write learners the time they need to dig in.

Write on a board. You may want to consider using a whiteboard or tear-off notepad in your group gatherings. Ask someone to take notes during the discussion so the primary ideas and opinions being shared are displayed for everyone to see.

Give tests and evaluations. Again, this probably won't be a popular feature for your group, especially if you do it every week. But there's value in writing up a little quiz before your group begins a new curriculum series to see what the members already know. And there's value in another quiz or evaluation after the series is finished to see what they've retained. Your read/write learners will also like it if you set up a game based on the TV show *Jeopardy!* or the board game Trivial Pursuit.

Kinesthetic Learners

People with a kinesthetic learning style (also called a tactile learning style) prefer to process information through their fingers and skin. They're "hands on" and would choose to participate in physical activities rather than listen to a lecture or participate in a debate. They learn well when they can manipulate physical objects and conduct experiments.

Kinesthetic learners usually don't like trying to explore abstract theories or ideas. They prefer to be more concrete and practical. "Practice makes perfect" would be an ideal motto for a kinesthetic learner. They also place a high value on experience. They hold something to be more true if they've experienced it, and they would prefer others to tell stories about their experiences rather than give opinions on matters for which they're not experts.

Here are some other cues and clues that may help you recognize a kinesthetic learner:

> If you ask a kinesthetic learner for directions, she just may offer to take you to the destination herself.
> When a kinesthetic learner orders food at a restaurant, he prefers to choose something he's eaten at that restaurant before—a dish he's already experienced.
> A kinesthetic learner would rather hold a book in her hand than read something from a screen. She may also trace her finger along the page as she reads.
> Kinesthetic learners enjoy sports and other activities that allow them to engage their bodies with the world around them. Gardening is a good example.

> A kinesthetic employee would prefer to watch his boss demonstrate what needs to be done than read a manual or listen to his boss explain the task.
> If you've heard of a child taking apart a telephone or alarm clock and then trying to put it back together, that child was probably a kinesthetic learner.
> Kinesthetic learners use words and phrases like these: *application*, *get my hands dirty*, *that feels right*, and *it's been my experience that*.

KINESTHETIC LEARNERS IN GROUPS

Many aspects of participating in a group are unappealing to kinesthetic learners. First and foremost is staying seated in the same place for a long period of time. The traditional method of "going around the circle" for prayer requests is also disagreeable for kinesthetic learners because it takes so long for everyone to talk about what's on their mind and then for everyone to pray out loud.

Kinesthetic learners can also become frustrated when a group spends most of its time talking, discussing, and debating. They want to move quickly into application. They want to get out of the living room and do something.

Here are some ways you can improve the experience of kinesthetic learners in your group:

Do service projects. Kinesthetic learners are great for groups because they're often the ones pushing others to "practice what they preach." They want to get out into the world and make an impact based on what the group's been learning. So make service projects part of the group's experience.

Establish mentoring relationships. Paul's admonition to "follow my example, as I follow the example of Christ" (1 Cor. 11:1) sounds just right to kinesthetic learners. Rather than establish some kind of vague accountability within the whole group, kinesthetic learners do well when they can be in a *Do as I do* relationship with another disciple of Jesus—both as the mentor and the mentee.

Move around. Sitting still is not preferred for kinesthetic learners, so build in some activities that provide people a chance to move their bodies. Announce a stretch break for five minutes before the discussion starts. Encourage people to get down on their knees or walk around during prayer time.

Give them something to hold. A kinesthetic learner will do much better during a "sit and talk" activity if they have something to hold, squeeze, bend, or throw. Consider making one or more of these materials available at each group meeting: a small rubber ball, pipe cleaners, Play-Doh, a Rubik's Cube—anything that can be physically manipulated while a person sits and participates in a discussion.

Multimodal Learners

In addition to a dominant learning preference, most people feel comfortable perceiving and processing information through at least one other learning style—what's called a "secondary" learning style. Neil Fleming referred to these individuals as multimodal learners, and his research indicates that more than half of people who take the VARK questionnaire demonstrate at least one secondary learning style.[4]

Many multimodal learners act as if they have two, three, or even four dominant learning styles, meaning they can switch back and forth between their preferences in order to best match the information to be learned.

I am a read/write learner, for example, but I also have a secondary kinesthetic learning preference. When my lawnmower breaks, which seems to happen every summer, I'm comfortable with trying to diagnose the problem by taking the engine apart and looking for something out of place. This is a kinesthetic approach. I find this more efficient than reading about potential problems and then taking the engine apart, which would be the read/write approach.

Some multimodal learners aren't able to switch back and forth between learning styles but instead attempt to gather and process information using several styles at once. These individuals often learn at a slower pace because they have to synthesize different types of information gleaned from different types of sources. When they complete the process, however, they often have a tighter grip on what they've learned than others who operate in one style at a time.

All in all, the presence of multimodal learners is good news for group leaders. That's because group members with a multimodal preference are able to learn in more than one way, which means they feel more comfortable in a greater number of activities during a group meeting.

Social and Solitary Learners

In addition to the four learning styles included in the VARK model, people also prefer learning in either a social or solitary environment.

There's not a lot to explain with these terms. Social learners prefer to be around other people. They learn best when they can talk with or participate in activities with other people. They seem to gain energy when they're in a crowd of people, and they're less motivated to learn when they're alone.

Solitary learners are just the opposite. Given a preference, they prefer to perceive and process information by themselves, and they retain that information best when they don't have many distractions around them. Solitary learners can "burn the midnight oil" reading by themselves or taking apart a complicated machine, but they become drained when they're expected to be part of a crowd for more than a short amount of time.

Obviously, a group setting is better suited for social learners.

And that probably means a large percentage of people in your group are social learners. If you give them opportunities to connect, talk, and experience the group together, they'll be happy.

Most solitary learners won't have a problem being part of a small group for one or two hours each week—they aren't hermits who never want to be exposed to other human beings. But it's true that social environments are not the ideal place for them to learn new ideas and concepts or accurately process different experiences.

So here are some things you can do to assist the solitary learners in your group:

Allow for homework. Again, some people really do prefer to study and engage a book or curriculum guide during the week. For solitary learners, the chance to get acquainted with the discussion material by themselves will limit the amount of distraction they feel when participating with the whole group.

Create subgroups. It's often a good idea to split your group into smaller subgroups, with each subgroup containing two to four people. This provides a more intimate experience for prayer, worship, or discussion. And for solitary learners, it minimizes potential distractions and doesn't drain their energy as quickly as a larger group would.

Minimize the pressure. Small groups in general are viewed as a social experience, which means people are expected to "pitch in" and "get involved." For that reason, many group leaders become nervous when one or two people don't say much in a group, or when those people leave right after the group ends instead of staying to chat. But those behaviors are natural for a person with a preference toward solitary learning. So don't apply a lot of pressure aimed at getting everyone to participate on an equal basis. Let solitary learners ease in at their own pace.

Engaging Multiple Learning Styles in a Small Group

If you have a mind for math, I can guess what you're probably thinking right now: *Let's see . . . Four dominant learning styles, plus multimodal learners, plus a choice between solitary or social learning. That's dozens of possible combinations when it comes to the learning preferences in my group! How in the world can I plan for all those?*

Believe me, the last thing I want to do is make life more difficult or meeting preparation more time-consuming for group leaders. But thankfully, preparing for each group meeting in a way that engages all the learning styles your group members might have requires only two steps.

STEP 1: CHECK FOR GAPS

First, review your Bible study plan or curriculum guide and identify which learning styles will be targeted throughout the session. For example, if you're using a Bible study that opens with an icebreaker activity where people get up and walk around, you'll know that activity will appeal to kinesthetic learners. Then if, later on, the study contains several questions to help you facilitate a discussion, you'll know that will appeal to auditory learners.

You'll want to make a mental note of these connections at the very least. But I recommend you take it a step further and write a *K* next to the icebreaker and an *A* next to the discussion questions. That way you have a quick reminder that the kinesthetic and auditory learning styles have been targeted.

Note: It's possible for one segment of the curriculum guide to appeal to multiple learning styles at the same time. For example, an icebreaker where all your group members walk around and talk to each other about their childhood memories would connect with kinesthetic, auditory, and social learners. So you would write *K*, *A*, and *Social* next to that icebreaker.

When you finish reviewing the study, just look back and see how many times each learning style has been targeted. More importantly, check to see which learning styles have not been targeted.

If you don't see any *V*s, for example, you know there's a gap in that Bible study for visual learners. If you see ten *A*s, that means the study is overbalanced toward auditory learners.

STEP 2: FIND A BALANCE

Once you've identified the gaps in a given Bible study or curriculum guide, take a few moments to plan additional elements or activities that fill in those gaps.

For example, I mentioned before that a lot of prewritten curriculum guides do a poor job of appealing to visual learners. If that's the case with your particular study, try to find a video clip that connects with the topic of discussion. Or household objects that can provide a visual association to doctrines or concepts, like a pair of scissors to show the need to cut sin out of our lives or a loaf of bread to remind us that the Bible is part of our spiritual nourishment.

In a similar way, pay attention if your study guide has an imbalance toward one or more learning styles. For example, I mentioned that marking ten *A*s shows that a study is pretty heavily favored toward auditory learners. In that situation, just cross out a few of the elements that don't seem necessary. Plan on skipping them in favor of a more balanced approach.

One of the best ways to maintain a balanced approach to your preparation for each group meeting is to emphasize the use of icebreakers and learning activities. That's because they often appeal to multiple learning styles. The key is to connect these icebreakers and activities with the central topic of the group's discussion, which I discuss in detail throughout Part Two.

Another way to maintain a balanced approach in your lesson preparation is to add layers to the existing elements already in your Bible study. Instead of thinking up a whole new activity that would appeal to kinesthetic learners, just add a layer of physical movement to something that's already part of your plan. Have people toss a ball back and forth during the discussion time, for example. Whoever is holding the ball has the floor to speak, and that person can toss the ball to the next person with something to say.

Finally, if you feel like the study is fairly balanced without your doing any extra work, that's great. You're golden. Don't spend any more time on this than you have to.

AN IMPORTANT PUBLIC SERVICE ANNOUNCEMENT

I don't want to end this chapter without making one thing clear: *group leaders should not try to make every part of a group meeting appeal to all possible learning styles.* That's not a realistic goal, and it wouldn't be very helpful even if you were able to achieve it.

As I mentioned before, every person in your group has the capacity to perceive and process information through all four of the VARK learning styles. Yes, each group member has a dominant learning style they prefer to operate in. Yes, it's likely that group members will become bored, uncomfortable, or disconnected if they sit through an entire group meeting without any connection to that dominant learning style. But that's all they really need: a connection. A taste. A chance to operate in their element here and there.

So concentrate on leading your group through gatherings that are balanced as a whole. Give your group members one or two experiences each meeting that allow them to think and learn in the ways most natural to them. Doing so will go a long way toward creating an environment where the Holy Spirit can operate and each person can grow.

PART 2

Planning
Your Route

I've led more than a thousand group meetings, and I can
honestly say I've engaged in some form of preparation for
every one of them.

Sometimes that preparation has been thorough, involving commentaries and concordances and hours of extra work. Other times
it's been hurried and harassed—scribbling notes and Scripture ref-
erences on scratch sheets of paper as the first group member pulls
into the driveway. Mostly it's been somewhere in the middle.

In many ways, each act of preparing for a group meeting has
been an experience unique unto itself. Each one involved a different
combination of material to explore, including Scripture passages
and books other than the Bible, plus a different collection of group
members to join me in the exploring.

But I've also developed a general routine that I follow as I prepare
for group gatherings week in and week out. This routine includes

a handful of activities that help me map out a plan for each group meeting—a strategy that lets me determine ahead of time where I hope to go and what I hope to accomplish.

The five chapters in Part Two of this book are designed to give you an overview of those activities so you can develop your own plan for each group meeting:

> Chapter 6 introduces the "big idea" as an important part of preparing for and leading a group meeting.
> Chapter 7 offers advice on using icebreakers and learning activities.
> Chapter 8 explains how to write discussion questions that actually spark discussion.
> Chapter 9 examines what's required when preparing for times of worship and prayer within your group meetings.
> Chapter 10 helps you put everything together in a final plan and explains the danger of unintended curriculum.

Chapter 6

The Big Idea

Take a moment to consider another scenario involving Crush, our fictional safari guide.

Crush gathers your group together and, thankfully, leads you into the jungle this time. You begin walking down a narrow path, and Crush shares some interesting facts about various plant species you find along the way.

After a few minutes, someone in your group asks Crush if any monkeys populate this part of the jungle, and he answers yes. He even offers to lead everyone to a tribe of howler monkeys living nearby. Along the way, however, another group member spots a brightly colored lizard, which Crush unsuccessfully attempts to catch for several minutes. The chase has led your group off the path, but Crush knows a shortcut to the howler monkeys, and he strikes off with everyone in tow.

Suddenly, a parrot lands on a nearby branch, and Crush launches into an extended and detailed explanation of its plumage and diet. This does not sit well with the group member who wanted to see the monkeys, and he scowls and loudly clears his throat in protest.

When the bird finally flies away, Crush leads the group on a long hike until you're within sight of the howler monkeys' main tree.

Unfortunately, Crush remembers too late that howlers are nocturnal, and so all you can see are a few fuzzy lumps sleeping peacefully among the branches.

Now there's no time left to strike off in search of other interesting creatures, so Crush leads you and the rest of the group back to the Jeep and back to your camp.

How would you feel about that safari experience? It could have been worse, certainly. You got to go into the jungle this time, and at least you saw some interesting animals. Yet the entire trek suffered from a lack of direction, which resulted in a lot of wandering coupled with only a few moments of interesting activity.

The same thing can happen in your group meetings if you don't commit to preparing a useable plan ahead of time. And your first step in preparing that plan should be to identify what I call a "big idea."

Defining Terms

The concept of a big idea is not difficult or complicated: the big idea is the main premise you want to explore with your group during a given meeting.

Here's another way to say it: *the big idea is the main principle you would want participants to remember from a gathering or discussion if you knew they would forget everything else.*

For example, imagine how the preceding safari scenario would have been different if Crush had determined ahead of time that his main goal was to help the group experience the tribe of howler monkeys. He could have incorporated information about the lizard and the parrot during the group's journey without allowing them to become a distraction. He also could have approached the monkeys in a way that allowed the group to experience them best. (Namely, closer to nightfall—but not so close that they're only fuzzy lumps.)

In the same way, you'll have the most success as a leader if you identify a specific idea or theme you want your group members to encounter during their time together. That theme can be as simple as telling the group, "We're going to explore the doctrine of grace." Or even "We're going to read Romans 3 and see how it applies to our lives." Your big idea can also be topical, especially if your group is studying a book. Something like, "We're going to talk about forgiveness in marriage."

The point is this: one of your main tasks as a group leader is to help your group members stay focused as they explore that idea or theme. It's your job to prevent the group from wandering around aimlessly, and having a big idea allows you to do that job well.

I want to make one more thing clear before I go any further: working with a big idea shouldn't be overly complicated or time-consuming. It shouldn't be a burden or an obstacle you have to overcome during the process of preparing for a group meeting. Rather, a big idea is a simple decision that helps you stay focused as you prepare for and lead a group meeting. It's the difference between saying, "We're going to eat dinner at Joe's Crab Shack" and "We're going to drive around downtown and see if we can find a place to eat."

The Educational Benefits of a Big Idea

Beyond sharpening your focus, having a big idea will also provide an educational benefit for your group meetings. That's because everyone attending those meetings (including you) will be a human being, and human beings are controlled by human brains. And most human brains have a hard time processing and retaining a large amount of information in a small amount of time.

Here's a quick experiment to show you what I mean. Think back to the last time you attended a worship service at your church. (I'm talking about the Sunday-morning experience with the senior pastor and a parking lot, not a small group meeting.) See if you can answer these questions in connection with that service:

> What did you eat for breakfast that morning?
> Can you name three people you talked to before, during, or after that service (not including your family)?
> How many songs did the worship team lead?
> What was the main Scripture reference in your pastor's sermon?
> How many of your pastor's bullet points can you remember?

If you're feeling good about your answers, keep moving back in time. Can you answer those questions about the sermon you attended two weeks ago? A month ago? I can't either.

The same experiment can work with the last group meeting you were part of, assuming it was recent:

> Who was the first person to arrive at the meeting (also assuming you were the host)?
> Can you name three prayer requests group members other than you (or your family) made?
> Which concepts most interested you during the discussion?
> Can you answer the same questions about a group meeting you participated in more than a month ago?

Here's the reality: people forget the majority of what they hear from their pastor during each week's sermon. And they forget the majority of what they hear and discuss during your group meetings. This happens because those events are usually packed with more information than you or I can reasonably process and retain over time.

I remember one gathering where our group spent fifteen minutes talking about justification. I had prepared a definition beforehand, and several people worked through the doctrine in their own words—how it applied to salvation, how it was different from sanctification, and so on. The very next week I was introducing the idea that Abraham was justified by faith (Romans 4) when someone who'd been present the previous week asked, "What does *justified* mean?"

That was frustrating. I put a lot of effort into planning those group meetings, after all—a lot of time and energy. It was deflating to learn that this group member wasn't retaining much of what we discussed, and I soon realized that person wasn't alone. I felt like giving up.

Maybe you're feeling the same way right now. But giving up and canceling your group is not a good solution to this problem. Neither is trying to "dumb things down" so your group members won't forget the majority of what's discussed. No, the answer is to help your group members understand, retain, and apply the most important elements of each group meeting.

What you can do is structure each gathering so your people are confronted with one vital principle over and over, which gives them more opportunities to engage and interact with that principle. It also provides more opportunities for the Holy Spirit to make an impact in your group and help everyone, you included, retain that principle and apply it to your lives in a way that produces spiritual growth.

That is why you need a "big idea."

How to Identify the Big Idea

Identifying a big idea for a particular group meeting involves just two steps:

1. Read through (or watch) the material to be covered in that meeting.
2. Pick a direction from that material that best fits the needs and current trajectory of your group.

If you're writing a Bible study from scratch, the material you need to read through is the Scripture passage(s) for the group meeting plus whatever supplemental resources you plan on using, like books, commentaries, websites (more on that soon). If you're using a book or prewritten curriculum, you'll need to read through that as well.

One nice thing about prewritten curriculum is that the authors usually do a lot of spadework for you in terms of approaching the group meeting in an organized way. In my review of study guides in recent years, I've found more and more studies that provide a central theme or idea for each group session—usually you find it in the introductory material or even in the title. If that's the case, chances are good that this theme will serve as your big idea (although you may want to tweak it to match the specific needs of your group).

Even if your curriculum doesn't have a central theme, most study guides provide from two to five main points for each session, with discussion questions and activities divided between those points. That gives you a solid road map of the concepts that will be up for discussion, and you can create your own big idea by finding the common element between those main points or by focusing on one or two main points and eliminating the rest.

A Quick Word about Research

Part of the process of identifying a big idea is becoming familiar enough with the material to make educated decisions about what you want to happen during a group meeting. And that usually means doing a bit of research, especially if you're writing your own curriculum. Commentaries, sermons, footnotes, and everything in between are useful in sparking ideas and helping you focus your thoughts. But the question I often hear from group leaders is this: "How much research is enough?"

There's no easy way to answer that question. Some group leaders go crazy, reading supplementary materials for hours in preparation for a group meeting. Others don't read anything except the Bible verses that will be under discussion. My general opinion is that the best approach lies somewhere in the middle.

I like to have Bible study tools available to answer questions that occur to me as I read the text. And I do read commentaries to get a sense of what the experts think about any Scripture passages to be featured in a group meeting. But I almost always read commentaries last so I can gather my own thoughts instead of defaulting to whatever the experts say. Altogether, I rarely spend more than twenty or thirty minutes reading "outside" material in preparation for a group meeting.

Really, the point of adding research to your preparation for a group meeting is to help you feel more confident in your understanding of the material to be explored. You want to make sure you're not turning your back on basic doctrines or reading more into a text than is actually there. You also want to gain some information about the context of your Scripture passages so you can pass some of that along to your group members and have a shot at answering some of the questions they ask.

One more thing about research before a gathering: look for quality sources. Google and Wikipedia are wonderful tools, but a lot of the material available on the internet is questionable—bad theology and lazy opinions that can knock both you and your group off track. Published books don't always contain helpful or accurate information either, but at least most of them have gone through a process of peer review.

The best thing to do is find an author or series of resources you connect with and trust—especially ones recommended and approved by scholars and theologians. Your pastor can also be a trusted resource.

Case Study

Throughout the rest of Part Two, I spend a portion of each chapter recreating the steps I took to prepare for a group meeting that focused on James 3:1-12. (Think of it as an extended case study.) In order to maintain consistency, all examples refer to the same portion of Scripture, and I carry the progress from each chapter to the next.

My first step in preparing for that group meeting was to read through the source material and identify a big idea. So here is the text, James 3:1–12:

> Not many of you should become teachers, my fellow believers, because you know that we who teach will be judged more strictly. We all stumble in many ways. Anyone who is never at fault in what they say is perfect, able to keep their whole body in check.
>
> When we put bits into the mouths of horses to make them obey us, we can turn the whole animal. Or take ships as an example. Although they are so large and are driven by strong winds, they are steered by a very small rudder wherever the pilot wants to go. Likewise, the tongue is a small part of the body, but it makes great boasts. Consider what a great forest is set on fire by a small spark. The tongue also is a fire, a world of evil among the parts of the body. It corrupts the whole body, sets the whole course of one's life on fire, and is itself set on fire by hell.
>
> All kinds of animals, birds, reptiles and sea creatures are being tamed and have been tamed by mankind, but no human being can tame the tongue. It is a restless evil, full of deadly poison.
>
> With the tongue we praise our Lord and Father, and with it we curse human beings, who have been made in God's likeness. Out of the same mouth come praise and cursing. My brothers and sisters, this should not be. Can both fresh water and salt water flow from the same spring? My brothers and sisters, can a fig tree bear olives, or a grapevine bear figs? Neither can a salt spring produce fresh water.

As I read through the passage several times, I filtered out some of the major concepts and ideas it addresses:

- responsibility for teachers
- control
- the tongue
- speaking and using words
- good and evil
- danger/poison
- praising and cursing
- hypocrisy

Any of these themes would have made an interesting and potentially helpful big idea, especially if I wanted the group to concentrate on a smaller section of Scripture. For example, I could have focused on verses 1 and 2 and condensed the meeting to an exploration of the role and responsibility of teachers. But I chose to delve into all twelve verses, which required a broader big idea.

Here's what I eventually came up with: *the words we speak can accomplish powerful things for good and evil.* That was the main idea I wanted to explore with the members of my group during that particular meeting. If we didn't accomplish anything else, I wanted us to at least grapple with that truth.

Incidentally, it's common to find several good options for a big idea as you begin to explore the material for a group meeting—especially if you're looking at a book or passage of Scripture as diverse as James 3. In those situations, you have to make a choice based on what will be most applicable and helpful for your group.

If my group had spent several weeks studying the doctrine of sin, for instance, I may have chosen to focus the meeting on why the tongue is "a world of evil among the parts of the body."

In the end, identifying a big idea will provide considerable dividends throughout your preparations for a group meeting—as you'll see in the remaining chapters of Part Two.

Chapter 7

Icebreakers and Learning Activities

I was skimming through the book of Revelation in preparation for another group meeting when I came across this verse: "Wake up! Strengthen what remains and is about to die, for I have found your deeds unfinished in the sight of my God" (Rev. 3:2).

I really liked the impact of those first two words: "Wake up!" And they gave me an idea for a good way to start the discussion on that chapter. So at the beginning of our next group meeting, I told everyone I had a challenge to announce: "I'll give five dollars to anyone who can fall asleep in the next five minutes. Any takers?"

Of the two volunteers, one laid on the floor, and the other tried to snuggle into his corner of the couch. While they attempted to lose consciousness, I asked the other members of the group to talk about the rituals they went through each night as they prepared for bed.

When five minutes had passed, I said, "I'd like everyone who's awake to please raise their hand." Both volunteers sat up and put their hand in the air—accompanied by a few good-natured jeers from the other group members, of course. (Not from me, though. I was just thankful to be keeping my money.)

After everyone calmed down a bit, I asked the volunteers, "What happened? Can either of you explain why you weren't able to fall asleep?" They had similar answers. They were distracted by the conversation from the rest of the group, and their minds were overly active because they couldn't stop thinking about falling asleep. One of them actually said, "It's easy to wake up on command, but not the other way around."

That was my cue to say, "Well, thanks to both of you for trying. Now let's all open our Bibles to Revelation 3, and we'll look at an entire church that was commanded to wake up."

In my opinion, that story demonstrates an effective use of a learning activity (in this case an icebreaker) to supplement the discussion portion of a group meeting. I'll explain why I think so in the rest of this chapter—and offer some tips and techniques to help you plan similar activities for your own group.

Defining Terms

The first thing I want to make clear is that I view *learning activity* and *icebreaker* as similar terms yet slightly different.

Learning activity is the broader term, encompassing any educational activity within a group meeting that goes beyond discussion. So learning activities have two key characteristics:

1. They're educational, which means they're intended to help you and the other members of your group interact with truths and ideas that can be learned.
2. They go beyond discussion, which means they involve more than talking or debating about those truths and ideas. Learning activities incorporate additional attributes, such as physical movement, artistic expression, humor, and competition.

That means all kinds of activities can be considered "learning activities" within a group meeting. Examples include games, role play, object lessons, drawing, music, and making crafts. Even something as crazy as trying to get group members to fall asleep can work well as a learning activity within the boundaries of a group. Because they help people with different learning styles engage in the topics being explored by the group, this diversity makes learning activities an invaluable element of group meetings. As I mentioned in chapter 5, people with an auditory learning style would generally be happy to spend one or two hours talking about important issues and ideas. But visual, read/write, and kinesthetic learners need to go beyond discussion in order to feel comfortable and engaged. Learning activities help them do that.

In addition, most learning activities provide an opportunity for fun. They let group members interact with each other in diverse and creative ways that go beyond sitting and talking, which is usually enjoyable.

In terms of frequency, I almost always plan at least one learning activity for each group meeting I lead (usually as an icebreaker), but I seldom plan more than two.

Exploring Icebreakers

An *icebreaker* is a specific type of learning activity that occurs at the beginning of a group meeting or the discussion portion of a group meeting. Icebreakers serve an introductory role, meaning they move people toward the truths and ideas to be explored (whereas a general learning activity could be a way of interacting with an idea or truth after it's already been introduced).

I want to zero in on icebreakers for a moment, because I place a high value on their use within groups. In fact, I incorporate an icebreaker into the beginning of every group meeting I lead, and I've done so for years.

Beyond appealing to multiple learning styles and allowing for fun, icebreakers offer three unique benefits to group leaders.

1. **Icebreakers provide a transition from the outside world.** It would be great if every person walked into a gathering ready to be an A+ participant—fully engaged with the study material and eager to participate. But that doesn't always happen. Maybe Steve walks in feeling stressed because he had a rough day at the office. Or Mary and James have a six-month-old who doesn't sleep through the night, which means they're both exhausted. Or Sheila is still thinking about the end of a fascinating movie she just saw.

   In reality, everybody who attends your group meeting brings with them the potential for serious distraction—including you. But an icebreaker helps people transition from those distractions into the life of the group. It allows them to focus on something creative, humorous, or physical, which begins to take their attention away from whatever was happening "outside" and helps them focus on being present "inside."

2. **Icebreakers trigger engagement.** Do you remember learning about Pavlov's famous experiment with dogs? Ivan Pavlov was a physiologist who used a variety of stimuli (including ringing a bell) whenever he brought food to a select group of dogs. Pretty soon the dogs began to salivate whenever he rang that bell regardless of whether or not he had food. The ringing bell triggered a specific response.

   A similar thing can happen with icebreakers—although it shouldn't involve drooling. When you consistently begin your group meetings with an icebreaker, your group members will quickly normalize that experience. They'll expect it; they'll anticipate it. More importantly, they'll connect the icebreaker to the other elements of your group time. Just like Pavlov's dogs connected the ringing bell with eating, your group members will connect the experience of an icebreaker with relational connection, discussion, worship, prayer, and application. This means the icebreaker will trigger your group members to prepare for engagement in those activities. Without thinking about it, they'll open up relationally. Their minds will begin to focus in preparation for discussion. They'll begin to think about God in preparation for prayer and worship. In other words, they'll get ready to fully engage in the activities of the group meeting.

3. **Icebreakers encourage people to arrive on time.** Many group leaders start their meetings with anywhere from ten to thirty minutes of fellowship time. This can be a good practice, but it can also train people to arrive late. If your group is supposed to start at 7:00 p.m., for example, some members will begin arriving at 7:10 or 7:15. They'll think, *It's not a big deal; I'm just missing a little bit of fellowship time.*

But pretty soon they'll plan on arriving at 7:15, and then one day something will happen that makes them arrive later than they planned, and they'll enter the meeting at 7:30. When this starts happening to several of your group members, punctuality becomes a big problem.

Using an icebreaker at a specific time in every gathering—at 7:15, for example—is a great way to contend with this issue. Doing so provides group members with both a positive incentive for arriving on time (icebreakers are interesting and fun) and a negative incentive for arriving late (missing the icebreaker means missing the introduction to the meeting's theme).

As you can probably tell, I'm a big fan of icebreakers and their utility within a group meeting. But there is one challenge: the icebreaker needs to be good. It needs to be written or framed in a way that actually accomplishes what you want it to accomplish.

Because of my experiences in the world of small groups, I've had the opportunity to read and evaluate a large number of the Bible studies and curriculum guides available for group leaders to purchase. And while many of these resources contain useful material, very few of them offer group leaders any help when it comes to the kinds of learning activities described in this chapter.

True, many Bible studies do provide an icebreaker at the beginning of each session, but most of them consist of a single question designed to be answered by each person in the group. "What was your favorite color as a child?" for example. Or "If you could go on vacation anywhere in the world, where would you go?"

Sometimes the question may involve multiple choices. *If God made you an animal instead of a human being, what would you be?*

> ➤ a lion
> ➤ a mouse
> ➤ a sloth
> ➤ a whale
> ➤ a bee

To be fair, these kinds of questions can provide some valuable insights at the beginning of a group's journey together. They can help people get to know each other through sharing stories, dreams, and fears. But in my experience these icebreaker questions quickly become stale. I remember using the *What was your favorite color as a child?* question with one of my earlier small groups. As we went around the circle, participants gave one-word answers with the efficiency of a machine gun: "Red." "Green." "Yellow." "Yellow." "Pink." "Green." "Purple." "Blue."

I struggled for thirty seconds or so to think of a follow-up question, and for a moment I was on the verge of asking, "Well, what's your favorite color now?" Mercifully, I thought better of it and dove into the discussion questions instead.

Sadly, as barren as published curriculum can be in terms of robust and helpful icebreakers, the landscape is positively desolate when it comes to providing additional learning activities within a study. Honestly, I can count on two hands the number of curriculum guides I've seen that included any kind of learning activity in the middle of or at the end of a session.

Here's what that means: if you want to include full-bodied icebreakers or learning activities within your group meetings, you'll probably have to come up with them yourself. And that's true even if you purchase a published Bible study.

Don't be afraid, though. Developing effective icebreakers and learning activities is much easier than it may seem at first—especially after you practice a few times and start getting the hang of it.

To that end, I spend the rest of this chapter highlighting the key steps in the process of creating helpful learning activities, along with a few techniques that have served me well week in and week out. To aid this process, I continue the case study from James 3 I began in chapter 6.

Step 1: Identify Core Concepts

Earlier, I mentioned that one of the main benefits of using learning activities in a group meeting is that they help you and your group members explore key concepts more deeply. Therefore, the first step in developing an effective learning activity is to identify the key concepts you'd like to explore in a given meeting.

Returning to the analogy of group leaders as spiritual safari guides, this act of identifying core concepts would be like choosing the specific animals you plan to visit during an excursion into the jungle. You're making a rough map of the truths and ideas you hope to interact with during a group meeting. The good news is that you may have already completed this step while identifying a big idea.

For example, as I said before, in the case study I started in chapter 6 I identified the following major concepts while exploring James 3:1-12:

> responsibility for teachers
> control
> the tongue
> speaking and using words
> good and evil
> danger/poison
> praising and cursing
> hypocrisy

Any of these concepts would make an interesting foundation for a learning activity. But that can create another problem—how to decide which core concept(s) should be explored through a learning activity. After all, it might be fun to develop a group meeting with eight distinct learning activities, but that wouldn't leave much room for anything else.

This potential problem can be solved in two ways. The first is to go broad and create a learning activity that addresses several core concepts at once. You can create one based on the big idea, for example, which usually works well as an icebreaker.

The second solution is to choose a specific core concept based on need. Using the major concepts I discovered in James 3:1–12, I might have created a learning activity that focused on "praising and cursing" if I felt my group members would be especially interested in that topic—or if I was using a prewritten curriculum that failed to address it.

As it happened, I chose the first solution. I decided to create a learning activity (an icebreaker, in this case) that would introduce the big idea at the beginning of the group meeting.

Step 2: Identify a Basic Activity

So I wanted to create an icebreaker that highlighted the main theme for the group meeting: that the words we speak can accomplish powerful things for good and evil. My next step was to come up with some kind of activity that could be connected to that theme.

I wish I could say a scientific method for identifying these kinds of activities exists. But in my experience, at least, the process is all about brainstorming. It's a matter of mentally chewing on the theme you want to explore until something useful comes to mind.

Continuing the case study, my first instinct was to focus on words that can have both positive and negative meanings. Like when someone says, "That guy is bad to the bone!" That could be either a compliment or an insult. But I couldn't think of an activity to go along with that idea.

Then I became enamored with the idea of powerful words—the notion that words can carry a sense of heft and weight. I thought it would be fun for my group members to talk about words and phrases that had influenced them throughout the course of their lives—perhaps lines from a song, quotations from books or movie quotes, or words of wisdom spoken by a family member.

But it hit me that what I was thinking of involved only sitting and talking. I was close, but I wanted to create something more active, not a glorified discussion question.

In the end I decided to take several magazines to the group meeting, hosted by another member of the group. I let my group members take a few copies each and skim through them in search of powerful words. Then after five minutes or so, we went around the circle so everyone could read whatever powerful words they'd found.

Step 3: Add Layers as Needed

I've mentioned that learning activities are valuable because they appeal to people with different learning styles within a group meeting. But that's not the only benefit that comes from their diverse nature; learning activities also stimulate the individual members of your group on different levels.

I think of this in terms of an athlete "warming up" their muscles. When I played football, for example, we did a variety of drills at the beginning of every practice, like jogging laps, Pilates, pushups, and jumping jacks. The purpose of these drills was to get blood flowing to our different muscle groups and stretch our tendons so that our bodies would be prepared for more intense exercise later in the practice. In a similar way, learning activities can "warm up" group participants on several different levels at the same time. Here are some examples:

Physical movement. It's a good idea to get your group members up and moving around every now and then. Americans spend a lot of time sitting, and an activity that requires movement can get your group members' blood flowing and help them wake up.

Example: Play a game of Simon Says and have your group members spin around, do jumping jacks, flap their arms.

Intellectual awareness. Use learning activities to help group members warm up their minds. This is especially helpful when your group tackles study material or portions of the Bible that are deep and require serious thought.

Example: Challenge your group members to solve a riddle, or divide the group into teams and have them race to finish a Sudoku puzzle.

Emotional awareness. Some group members need a little help when it comes to processing emotions around other people. (This is especially true for men, as well as for victims of abuse.) You can provide that help by creating an activity that requires group members to tap into an emotional memory or situation.

Example: If your topic is experiencing grief or perhaps the hope of heaven, have group members draw a picture representing their last memory of a family member who passed away.

Spiritual awareness. Sometimes group leaders think that every element of a group meeting needs to be "spiritual." That isn't true—it's more than appropriate to play a game or talk about your favorite movies without Christianizing them. But it can be useful to help your group members extend their spiritual antennae during a group meeting.

Example: Incorporate elements of worship or prayer into a learning activity. Or have group members share their testimonies about coming to faith in Christ (as long as they feel comfortable doing so).

Relational awareness. If you don't have a fellowship time at the beginning of your group meetings, learning activities are a great way to strengthen the bonds of friendship between your group members. This should be done regularly.

Example: Lead the group in a team-building exercise, or play a social game like Apples to Apples or Taboo.

Creativity. Small groups often focus on information-based pursuits and activities. So it's a good idea to regularly use learning activities as an outlet for creativity. This will be appreciated by the members of your group who are more artistic and imaginative.

Example: Give each group member a tub of Play-Doh and have them make a sculpture representing faith. Or split up into three smaller groups and have each group write a psalm expressing praise to God.

Curiosity. Curiosity may have killed the cat, but there's no doubt that it serves as an excellent motivator of human beings. Curious people are engaged people, which makes curiosity an important element of learning activities.

Example: Incorporate trivia questions into a learning

activity, or learn a magic trick and see if your group members can figure out its secret.

Here's another public service announcement: don't attempt to create a learning activity that engages all these levels of experience at once. That's not necessary and would not be helpful. Rather, an effective learning activity will stimulate people anywhere from two to four levels.

So how does all this fit into the task of creating an effective learning activity? Well, once you've settled on a basic structure for your learning activity, see if you can add one or more layers to the experience to help participants warm up on more levels.

For example, look again at this unhelpful icebreaker question: *What was your favorite color as a child?* One reason this isn't effective as an icebreaker or learning activity is that its only real purpose is to get group members talking to each other. So it stimulates people on a relational level, and that's about it.

But what if you gave a ball to the first person answering the question, and then asked them to throw the ball to the person they want to give an answer next? That would eliminate the predictable "going around the circle" bit, and it would also add some physical movement to the activity—another level of stimulation. You could take it a step further and have group members describe one of their happiest memories from childhood instead of their favorite color. That would add a level of emotional stimulation.

That's the basic idea: *Can I modify this activity so it helps people engage in the group meeting on more and more levels?*

Look again at the icebreaker activity I created for James 3. Giving my group members a chance to hunt through magazines would stimulate their curiosity. Asking them to hunt for powerful words would stimulate them intellectually. And giving everyone a chance to read what they found (and explain why the words were powerful to them) would add a level of relational engagement.

So I had put together a robust activity that had the potential to stimulate my group members on several different levels. After some thought, though, I decided to add one more layer. I had several pairs of scissors and instructed my group members to cut out the examples of powerful words they found. I thought we could put together a collage if we had time, which we didn't. But using the scissors did help everyone engage in more physical movement.

Step 4: Prepare for "Unpacking"

The final ingredient for any learning activity is a step I call "unpacking"—or "debriefing."

When you create a learning activity, you're trying to help your group members fully engage the Bible passage or study material you'll be exploring together. You want them to be stimulated, to experience emotions, and to grapple with core truths in a new and exciting way.

Unpacking allows participants to take a deep breath and process what they just experienced. It's a brief time for reflection—a time for everyone to think about their emotions and their reactions to the core truths just uncovered.

The actual process for unpacking involves two steps: asking questions and observation. The first you can prepare for prior to a group meeting, but the second is more spontaneous.

ASKING QUESTIONS

I recommend that, after deciding what you'll ask group members to do during a learning activity, you jot down a few questions to help everyone quickly debrief. Just like the goal of discussion questions is to help people create a dialogue connected to a Scripture passage or topic, the goal of these unpacking questions is to spark a conversation where participants can reflect on their experiences during the learning activity. This should not become a long list—from two to four questions is the ideal number.

When I write these questions, I think of squeezing a lemon wedge into a glass of water. The goal is to squeeze every last drop out of the learning activity—to pull out every insight and experience that can benefit the group. For example, here are the unpacking questions I wrote for the learning activity about powerful words from James 3:

> ➤ Which words found by other group members did you find especially powerful? Why?
> ➤ Where do you often encounter powerful words as part of your everyday life?

Notice that these questions refer to what happened during the learning activity. But they also connect with the broader concepts addressed by that activity—in this case, how words have a powerful effect in our lives.

OBSERVATION

When it's time to actually lead your group through a learning activity, think of yourself as a small group anthropologist—be intentional about observing your group members as they participate. Specifically keep your eyes and ears open for two things: (1) group members who react strongly to the experience, and (2) actions or words that connect with the core concepts explored by the activity, including the big idea.

If you were to lead the "powerful words" activity, for example, you might see one of your group members writing down a quotation. Or someone might smile broadly or wince as they read words considered powerful. You might hear a comment like, "I wish someone would say that about me."

When you observe these kinds of reactions—anything that indicates a person is experiencing something at a deeper level or interacting with a core concept—make a mental note of it. You may even want to write it down if you've got pen and paper handy.

Then bring it up again once the activity has ended. Do this by stating what you observed and asking the group member if they want to comment any further. "Sally, you were really beaming when you read that obituary. Did anything in particular make you feel happy?" Or "Jim, what was it about that sentence that made you wish someone would say it to you?"

By doing this, you're giving group members a chance to open up and reveal something about themselves from below the surface. And the results can be surprising. I've seen several people in my groups disclose new details of their story in response to such questions. I've also seen learning activities spark interesting questions, discussions about difficult situations, and even confessions of sin.

It's worth noting that some group leaders aren't comfortable "calling out" their group members by name. I understand that. And in general, it's best not to put people on the spot with questions they might not know how to answer. For example, you wouldn't want to ask, "Jim, what other passages of Scripture talk about powerful words?"

Unpacking questions is different because you're simply asking group members to shed some light on the motivations behind their actions. It's not a matter of the person possibly getting a question wrong; it's a matter of whether they're willing to reveal those motivations.

That brings up another important point: this is not a time for psychoanalyzing your group members. Don't try to draw out a person's thoughts with repeated questions, and certainly don't try to force anyone to talk. You're simply observing a group member's reactions, stating what you observed, and then giving that group member a chance to reveal deeper—*if they're ready.* If group members decline your invitation, or they share something still on the surface, move on. Period.

Chapter 8

| _ _____ _|_ _____ _|

Crafting Great Discussion Questions

There aren't a lot of things that really irritate me, but one of them is tap water. Yes, tap water. That may sound silly, but I have a good reason.

See, after purchasing a home a few years back, we discovered that the tap water contained a bunch of extra minerals and particles, which meant we weren't supposed to drink it. I know that's a pretty common problem in households across the country, and not being able to drink the water in and of itself isn't a big deal.

What bothers me is that we *should* have been able to drink our tap water. In fact, we should have been reveling in it!

Several years earlier the city government had invested $22 million to build a state-of-the-art water purification and treatment plant just a few miles from our home. The facility is spread across forty acres of farmland and draws water primarily from a deep sandstone aquifer—not from Lake Michigan (which is an important detail in the suburbs of Chicago). It also features a top-of-the-line reverse osmosis system that distributes the water out into the community.

So the water itself was not the problem. Every day we received gallons and gallons of the best water money can buy. There was no problem with our "taps," either. My wife and I remodeled both the kitchen and the bathroom after we moved in, and we were sure to install high-quality sinks and spigots.

No, the trouble was with the pipes that provided the connection between our city's multimillion-dollar treatment plant and our home's fancy faucets. Those pipes were old, for one thing, and most of them were iron. But several years back a previous owner had replaced a few of them with copper. He meant well, I think, but he forgot to include a dielectric union between the old iron pipes and the new copper ones, which caused corrosion in several places.

The end result? When really good water sits in really bad pipes overnight, you get really bad water in your cup the next morning—no matter how new or clean your faucets are.

You may be experiencing something similar in your home—not with your tap water but with the dialogue and discussion in your group.

Think about it. Just about every group discussion starts with the best source material available: the Bible. Not only is it the bestselling book of all time, but it has literally changed the course of human history. It was inspired and delivered by God Himself, for crying out loud!

Plus, just about every group discussion puts the Bible in the hands of interesting and intelligent people. Maybe you're thinking, *Well, you haven't met my group members.* Ha-ha. But I'm willing to wager that every person in your group has a story to tell. And I'm willing to wager that the majority of your group members are capable of understanding what the Bible has to say and capable of putting it into practice throughout their lives.

So if we have something interesting to discuss and interesting people to do the discussing, why are so many group meetings uninteresting?

The answer, or at least one of the answers, is bad discussion questions. They're the pipes that usually connect group members with God's Word—and with each other. And if those pipes are bad, the discussion will probably be bad as well.

The Different Types of Discussion Questions

Before I became a homeowner, I had no idea that a typical American home contains several different kinds of pipes—pipes for water, pipes for gas, and vent pipes just for air. Among those, you'll find pipes made of copper, iron, and galvanized steel. Several kinds of plastic pipes exist as well, from PVC to PEX. None of these materials is "better" than the others on a macrolevel. Rather, each type of pipe works best for a specific purpose. Taken all together, they form a complex system that keeps our houses running smoothly.

A similar dynamic is at play when it comes to discussion questions for your group. You need to be aware that there are several types of questions, and you need to be aware of how each type works best within the context of your group.

To that end, I spend the next few pages highlighting three broad patterns discussion questions often follow. Then I look at specific types of questions that reduce discussion and those that boost discussion and how to put together an effective series of questions while preparing for a group meeting.

In doing so, I also provide several example questions, all of which are based on James 3:1–12.

THE INDUCTIVE APPROACH

Studying the Bible has traditionally followed an inductive path made up of three steps: (1) observing what the text says, (2) interpreting what the text means, and (3) determining how the text can be applied. For that reason, many modern Bible studies and curriculum guides use three major categories of questions: (1) observation questions, (2) interpretation questions, and (3) application questions.

Observation questions focus on finding out what the text says. They're straightforward and can almost always be answered by looking back into the Scripture passage or other material being discussed. For this reason, observation questions are a good way to help your group identify information that will be useful later in the discussion. When used in moderation, they can also provide an easy way for people to chime in during a discussion.

Here are a few examples of observation questions:

> Why does James say "not many" believers should become teachers?
> What images does James use to describe the effects of the tongue?
> What part of the body is small yet makes "great boasts"?

Interpretation questions focus on what the text means. They give group members an opportunity to dig below the surface and think about why the Holy Spirit inspired a certain passage to be written—to identify the themes, ideals, principles, and commands it contains. Interpretation questions also provide an opportunity to explore textual context, historical context, and word definitions.

Here are a few examples of interpretation questions:

> What does James mean when he says teachers will be "judged more strictly"?
> Do the works of the tongue always result in evil? Why or why not?
> What is the significance of fresh water and salt water flowing from the same stream?

Application questions explore how the text is relevant to my life—and how I can respond to it. These questions are personal and targeted, which means they often begin with words like "How can you . . ." or "What will we . . ." Their goal is to challenge group members to make a commitment or take some kind of action in their regular lives outside of the group.

Application questions work well when they have a direct connection with one or more interpretation questions from earlier in the discussion. Meaning, after group members decide what a specific Scripture text means, the best application questions encourage them to do something about it.

Here are a few examples of application questions:

> How can we remain humble when we attempt to teach and lead others?
> What are some ways to fix the damage caused by our speech?
> What steps are we willing to take in order to minimize hypocrisy within our group?

OPEN VERSUS CLOSED

Any question you can write for a group meeting will fall into one of two camps: open or closed. Closed questions are easy to identify because they have only one correct answer. Once that answer has been identified, another question or statement is required in order for the conversation to continue.

For this reason, closed questions should be used sparingly within a group meeting. Too many of them will "close the door" on a meaningful discussion.

Still, I'm not advocating that closed questions be totally eliminated from group gatherings; they can be useful in certain situations. For example, they're an effective way to officially introduce a topic or piece of information into a discussion. They can also be helpful as a way to set up other questions better suited for sparking a conversation.

Here are two examples:

> What is the source of the "fire" contained within the tongue? (Introduces the topic of hell.)

> Can a fig tree bear olives? (Sets up the next question: How is it possible for followers of Jesus to produce harmful fruit with their words?)

Open questions are the opposite of closed questions in that they have several possible answers—none of which are necessarily right or wrong. For this reason, you want to focus on open questions as you prepare for a group meeting. Their presence will "open the door" to long and meaningful discussions.

"How is it possible for followers of Jesus to produce harmful fruit with their words?" is a good example of an open question. There's no single correct answer, and it can be explored through several different angles.

TEXT VS. EXPERIENCE

A third pattern often present in Bible studies and curriculum guides is the movement from text-based questions to experience-based questions.

Text-based questions are focused on whatever source material the group is studying—a passage of Scripture, a book, a speaker on a DVD or from a streaming service, a movie, and so forth. These questions shine a spotlight on that source material, allowing the group to dissect and debate its contents. Therefore, the discussions produced by them are usually impersonal and clinical; they're focused on the text rather than on the group members themselves.

On the other side of the coin are experience-based questions, which are focused on group members—their history and life experiences—instead of an "outside" text. The conversations produced by these questions are relational and sometimes deeply personal. Such questions are an important element in group meetings because they give group members a chance to share more about their stories.

Here are some examples of experience-based questions:

> What are some common characteristics of teachers who have made a positive impact on your life?
> What circumstances often result in losing control of your tongue?
> How do you react when you're confronted by hypocrisy in another person?

MIX AND MATCH

One reason I've highlighted these different patterns among discussion questions is to give you a sense of the options you have when preparing for a group meeting. There are many types of questions that can be asked, and being familiar with these patterns will help you achieve diversity in the questions you select.

Diversity is an important word when it comes to discussion questions. Having read through hundreds of Bible studies and curriculum guides in recent years, I've noticed that too many of them fall into common (and stale) routines.

Many studies are basically workbooks, for example. They're filled with closed observation questions—sometimes in the form of fill-in-the-blank sentences—punctuated by two or three application questions at the end. These guides work well for recording information and regurgitating doctrine, but they do little to produce actual discussion.

Other studies follow a strict inductive pattern. This starts with a large dose of observation questions (most of them closed), followed by several interpretation questions. Again, application questions are at the end. This is an efficient way to explore a passage of Scripture or a chapter in a book; however, they rarely move away from a text-based exploration and toward the experiences and stories of the people involved in the discussion.

I've found that by mixing and matching the different patterns of questions I've listed, you can add a richness and depth to your discussion experiences that's missing when all the questions feel the same, or when the group follows the same routine week after week. So be creative. Be diverse.

If you've written four interpretation questions in a row, add a question in the middle that allows group members to take a breather and talk about their personal experiences. Throw out an application question at the beginning of a discussion rather than always waiting until the end. (By the way, you might be surprised at how attempting to apply a truth will aid in the understanding of that truth.)

Questions That Kill Discussion

I mentioned earlier that closed questions have the potential to "close the door" on a meaningful discussion. Alas, they're not the only ones. Several types of questions can kill almost any discussion in just about any group.

I've listed some of the most common examples below.

IDIOTIC QUESTIONS

These questions have extremely obvious answers—so obvious that only an idiot could get them wrong.[1] Unfortunately, many group leaders are fond of these types of questions. The thinking is that they'll get people talking because everyone already knows the answer—thus sparking a discussion like using kindling will help start a fire.

The reality is that people aren't comfortable giving the answer to an obvious question. The idea of verbalizing something everyone already knows makes people feel silly (or even idiotic). As a result, idiot questions are usually followed by a long bout of awkward silence and sheepish glances until someone blurts out the answer in an effort to cut the rising tension. This effect is compounded when several idiot questions are asked together.

Here are a couple of examples:

> What do we put in the mouths of horses to make them obey us?

> Is it true that no human being can tame the tongue?

UNREASONABLE QUESTIONS

These questions fall at the opposite end of the spectrum in that their answers are unreasonably complicated or obscure. No one in the group will be able to answer them unless they speak Hebrew or have access to a Bible commentary.

Unreasonable questions often make their way into a group discussion when group leaders spend a lot of time in preparation and get a little overzealous about what they've learned.

Example:

> How would a first-century interpretation of the word *tongue* impact our understanding of this passage?

LONG-WINDED QUESTIONS

Sometimes the structure of a discussion question—the way it's written or the way it's asked—results in confusion among group members. This often happens when someone attempts to squeeze a lot of information into a question, causing it to be overly long, or when a question requires some extra explanation in order to be understood.

As with unreasonable questions, long-winded questions are often the by-product of overzealous preparation on the part of the group leader. In reality, people find it difficult to engage in a discussion when they don't understand what's being asked of them.

Here's an example of a long-winded question: "How do verses 11 and 12, which are rhetorical questions—a common literary device used in James's day—impact our understanding of the principle outlined in verses 9 and 10?"

I want to make it clear that providing extra information to your group members isn't always a bad thing. But when you find yourself in a situation where some context would be useful for your group members, I recommend just telling it to them in a straightforward way before you ask the next question.

Example:

> ➤ Rhetorical questions were a common literary device in James's day, and he uses three of them in verses 11 and 12. How do these questions impact our understanding of verses 9 and 10?

COMPOUND QUESTIONS

Compound questions are a variation of long-winded questions. Instead of packing a lot of information into a single query, group leaders sometimes stack three or more questions together, rapid fire, when those questions address a similar subject. (I also refer to this habit as "asking shotgun questions.")

Usually, someone will answer the last question in the series, and the preceding questions will be largely ignored.

Example:

> ➤ How does it make you feel to hear that teachers will be judged more strictly? Why do you feel that way? What qualifications for teachers are listed elsewhere in Scripture?

The solution is simply to break the string of questions apart and ask them one at a time.

"LEADING THE WITNESS" QUESTIONS

Some discussion questions are phrased in such a way that it's obvious the group leader is seeking a specific answer or wants to steer the discussion in a specific direction.

This is a bad idea for several reasons, not the least of which is the lack of respect demonstrated toward the other participants in the discussion. Group leaders who ask these kinds of questions behave like sheep dogs attempting to herd other people toward their way of thinking.

The bottom line is this: be wary of questions that contain any kind of built-in opinions.

Example:

> ➤ Does it seem like James is using hyperbole in verse 6, and what is his purpose in doing so?

The best way to fix "leading the witness" questions is to be honest about your opinions. (Even though you're the group leader, you're still allowed to share what you think.)

The good thing about bad questions is that they're easy to remedy. If you're developing a study from scratch, don't allow any of these insidious queries to creep into your material. To help with that, it's always good to perform a second edit on your work before the group gets together.

And if you find these kinds of questions in a prewritten Bible study, use a pen to scratch them out before the first group member even walks through your door. Remember, you hold the key to eliminating discussion-killing questions from your group.

Questions That Boost Discussion

All right. Enough about content that needs to be excluded from your gatherings. Several types of questions can produce a positive impact within a group discussion, and I've already mentioned two: open questions and experienced-based questions. Fortunately, we have many more.

As before, all example questions are based on James 3:1–12.

Crafting Great Discussion Questions   123

EMOTIONAL QUESTIONS

One way to avoid a discussion that focuses too much on the transfer of information is to include discussion questions that help people tap into their feelings and emotions.

Such questions don't have to be overly sentimental or dramatic—in fact, they shouldn't be. You just need to be sure that from time to time you're asking people to consider what they're feeling in addition to asking what they know.

Example:

> ➤ How do you react to the verse 2 claim that 'we all stumble in many ways'?

THOUGHTFUL QUESTIONS

I first heard about the "five minute rule" from Kevin Miller when he was a vice president at Christianity Today International. Kevin was giving a presentation to all the editors on our team when he said, "If an article comes across your desk that you're not sure of, ask yourself, *Could an average reader think of this on their own if they explored the topic for five minutes?*"

That's the "five minute rule," and I've found it to be helpful both as an editor and a group leader. I'm not saying that every discussion question you put before your group should be deeply thought-provoking or provocative. But some of them should be. After all, the goal of gathering as a group is to encounter God's Spirit in life-changing ways, and that usually doesn't happen when you keep discussion at the surface.

Examples:

> ➤ After reading 1 Timothy 1:3–11, keeping in mind James's warning in James 3:1, how can believers know when they're ready and able to become spiritual teachers?

➤ How much control can a human being gain over their tongue this side of eternity?

CONTROVERSIAL QUESTIONS

First, a note of caution: getting people stirred up to the point of arguing may result in an active discussion, but it rarely produces positive results—especially in terms of creating an atmosphere conducive to spiritual growth. So it's best to avoid asking contentious questions merely as a way to get people talking.

Still, controversial questions should have a place in your group meetings. That's because God's Word addresses several issues vital to the Christian life—like sin, salvation, miracles, money, and gender. Yet people don't always agree on what the Bible says regarding these issues. They're controversial topics, and helping your group explore them is part of honestly engaging the text.

Example (both controversial and helpful):

➤ Is it acceptable for followers of Jesus to denounce the sins of others? Why or why not?

FOLLOW-UP QUESTIONS

Group leaders are often told they need to be good at *facilitating* the discussions and interactions between their group members. That's an academic word, but all it really boils down to is knowing how to provide a spark or a little grease to your group's discussion when it begins to stall. And one of the best ways to serve as a facilitator is to ask follow-up questions.

These are spontaneous questions a group leader uses to gain clarification about a statement from a group member, to ask for more information, to seek out an illustration, or to open up a topic to the other people in the group.

Examples:

➤ "Dave, I hear you saying James is using hyperbole throughout these verses. Does everyone agree with that idea?"

➤ "Jim, what makes you say moving away from sarcasm was the hardest thing you've ever done?"

➤ "Susan, you mentioned that verses 11 and 12 are full of rhetorical questions. Why is that important?"

Creating an Effective Series of Discussion Questions

The remainder of this chapter addresses how to put together a series of discussion questions during the process of writing your own material. But I want to start with a few thoughts about tweaking the discussion questions you find in a prewritten or published Bible study.

First and foremost, you need to cut out whatever material doesn't fit with your group or your plans as the leader. And that definitely includes discussion questions.

Here's the reality: the vast majority of printed Bible studies I've seen contain way more discussion questions than a group would be able to address and answer in a single gathering—and that's on purpose. (I'll address this further in chapter 10.) It's your job to pick and choose the questions best suited for your group. Of course, if you come across any of the "discussion-killing" questions mentioned earlier, get rid of them.

Next, find any holes that need to be filled. Will any of the remaining questions approach your group members at an emotional level? Will they help them interact with and share their own stories? Do you see any deep, thoughtful questions? If not, you should probably add a few questions to balance out your session.

Okay, with that out of the way, let's explore some basic steps for creating an effective series of discussion questions to use with your group.

Note: the steps below apply primarily to situations where you're producing your own study plan and content rather than using a pre-written curriculum.

YOUR MOST IMPORTANT DISCUSSION QUESTION

I've mentioned several types and patterns of questions in this chapter. Most of them have value in the context of a group discussion. Yet I don't use any of them to start discussions in the group meetings I lead. I always use the same question to begin a group discussion—a question I believe is more important and useful than any other: "I want to get your initial reactions to the Scripture passage we'll be discussing in this gathering. What was surprising or significant or confusing about the text as you read through it?"

Of course, I use different phrases if the group will be focusing on a specific topic or the chapter of a book rather than a Scripture passage.

Many group leaders feel like they have to anticipate how their group members will react to a particular topic or section of the Bible in order to write effective discussion questions. Or they think they need to come up with a series of universal questions that will be universally interesting to each person in the group.

But stop and think about that for a moment. Isn't it a bit arrogant to expect our group members to talk for thirty to ninety minutes about the topics and questions we, the group leaders, find most compelling? At the least, it's biting off more than we can chew.

In my opinion, it's both much simpler and much more effective to allow group members to express what they find interesting, confusing, or significant and then follow that discussion as far as it will take you.

Of course, what your group members want to talk about might be different from the discussion topics and questions you had planned. And that's okay. It's more than okay, right? The whole point of gathering as a group is to interact with God's Word and each other in a way that creates life-changing experiences. If that means letting go of what you planned to talk about, so be it.

The only exception is when the group is moving far away from what you identified as the big idea. When that happens, you need to make a decision on the fly. Will you go with the flow and allow the group to determine the main topic, or will you rein in the discussion and return to your original big idea? That's a decision to be made in the moment, and you'll have to trust your instincts and experience to make it.

I realize taking this approach assumes your group members will read through the Bible passages or source material before the group gets together. And maybe you're thinking, *That won't happen with my group!* There's an easy way to fix this. I've found that reading the passage out loud as a group before the discussion starts is a great way to solve this problem—and a great habit to form anyway.

FREE WRITE THE NEXT SET OF QUESTIONS

Okay, now that you have your first and most important discussion question figured out, it's time to come up with some more. The best way to go about this is to write down every question that pops into your mind as you read through the Scripture passage or other material under discussion.

Don't be picky here, and don't try to weed out questions that won't work for the discussion. That comes later. This is just brainstorming.

IDENTIFY THE STRESS POINTS

The next step is to search for what I call the "stress points" within the text. These are the words and phrases that address weightier topics and ideas—the meat of a Scripture passage. In other words, these are the portions of the text that seem most interesting and important both for positive and negative reasons.

Positive stress points are words and phrases that provide explanations or highlight important truths. They may include:

Doctrinal statements. Some passages of Scripture serve as the basis or explanation for key doctrines of the Christian faith. These provide a great opportunity for education, discussion, and growth. For example, Ephesians 2:8–9 serves as a scriptural foundation for the doctrine of salvation by grace: "It is by grace you have been saved, through faith—and this is not from yourselves, it is the gift of God—not by works, so that no one can boast."

Commands. Because obedience and application are such important elements for spiritual growth, God-inspired commands recorded in the pages of Scripture are a great stopping point for discussion. Romans 12 contains a number of commands, for example, including verse 14: "Bless those who persecute you; bless and do not curse."

Commands are great material for group discussion because we usually need to do a bit of digging before we understand to whom the command applies. Are all Christians commanded to "bless those who persecute you," for example? Or was that only for the early Christians in Rome who received Paul's letter? That's a useful spark for conversation.

Promises. As with commands, when we discover a Spirit-inspired promise within the pages of Scripture, we should pay attention. Look at Matthew 17:20, for example: "Truly I tell you, if you have faith as small as a mustard seed, you can say to this mountain, 'Move from here to there,' and it will move. Nothing will be impossible for you."

Again, that's a great launching pad for discussion because it requires us to identify who is being addressed in addition to what is being said.

Visual elements. Visual elements embedded in Scripture passages will likely stand out to your group members—like word pictures, metaphors, visions, and poetic descriptions.

Next, let's look at negative stress points, which are verses or Scripture passages that may cause confusion or controversy within your group's discussion. They include:

Confusing words and phrases. Today, many resources to help us understand what biblical texts say and mean are available. Even so, a number of confusing passages remain. Like these verses from 1 Peter 3, which apply to Jesus: "After being made alive, he went and made proclamation to the imprisoned spirits—to those who were disobedient long ago when God waited patiently in the days of Noah while the ark was being built" (vv. 19–20). Chances are good that at least a few group members will get stuck on a passage like that, which makes it a great stopping point for group discussion.

Controversial texts. Some texts are more controversial than confusing. Different camps believe strongly in different interpretations and applications. A good example is 1 Timothy 2:12: "I do not permit a woman to teach or to assume authority over a man; she must be quiet."

Some people feel strongly that this command applies to all women in the church throughout all time; others feel strongly that it's limited to a specific culture (or even a specific church). Sharp lines are drawn, and that makes for controversy.

Be careful when you address controversial topics and Bible passages, however, because they carry the potential to produce frustration, bitterness, and even anger. People are more apt to fight about something when there's a well-defined disagreement rather than confusion.

Boring passages of Scripture. It's true. Many people find sections of the Bible boring—those long lists in the book of Numbers, for example, or the genealogy of Jesus in Matthew 1. And yet, strangely, those passages still have great potential for discussion within a group. That's because they allow you to ask *Why?* Why does the author include all these lists? Why is the same phrase repeated over and over? Why does Matthew spend so much effort making a connection between Jesus and Abraham?

It's exciting when a group begins to offer answers to some of these questions—like an archaeologist discovering valuable treasures in what looked at first like a pile of sand. That being said, sometimes you need to provide some outside information in order to spark those discoveries. So have a commentary or study notes available when you're preparing for a group meeting that will cover potentially boring material.

Continuing the case study, here are a few stress points I would identify from James 3:1–12:

> Verse 1 contains a promise, albeit a negative one: "We who teach will be judged more strictly."
> Verse 1 is also potentially confusing. What qualifies someone as a "teacher," for example? And why will teachers be judged more strictly?
> Verses 3–12 contain several visual elements, including metaphors (comparing the tongue with a rudder or with a fire) and strong images (horses, a ship, fire, several animals, springs of water).

Again, chances are good that your group members will zero in on one or more of these stress points during their own reading of the text, which means they're good material for discussion.

So check back over your brainstormed list of questions and see if any of them connect with the stress points you've identified. If so, you should give them strong consideration when you finalize your list of questions. And review the stress points to see if they spark other discussion questions you had not previously considered, then add those to the list.

Once you've got a good list of questions, use the big idea for the group meeting to winnow out any questions that don't support the main theme or idea you hope to explore. I do this by crossing out questions that have no connection with the big idea.

For example, here's a brainstormed list of questions based on James 3:1–12:

> ➤ Why will believers who teach be judged more strictly?
> ➤ What are some of the "many ways" you stumble in your walk as a Christian?
> ➤ Is it true that no human being can tame the tongue?
> ➤ How much control can a human being gain over their tongue this side of eternity?
> ➤ Is James using hyperbole in verse 6, or is he speaking literally?
> ➤ Can the tongue be used for good as well as for evil?
> ➤ Is it acceptable for followers of Jesus to denounce the sins of others? Why or why not?
> ➤ What songs or hymns are most effective in helping you connect with God?
> ➤ What does it mean that human beings are created in "God's likeness" (v. 9)?
> ➤ How do you interpret James's use of rhetorical questions in verses 11 and 12?

Remember, here's the big idea I'd established for the group meeting: *the words we speak can accomplish powerful things for good and evil.*

Here's what happens when I eliminate the questions that don't support that big idea:

- ~~Why will believers who teach be judged more strictly?~~
- ~~What are some of the "many ways" you stumble in your walk as a Christian?~~
- Is it true that no human being can tame the tongue?
- How much control can a human being gain over their tongue this side of eternity?
- Is James using hyperbole in verse 6, or he is speaking literally?
- Can the tongue be used for good as well as for evil?
- Is it acceptable for followers of Jesus to denounce the sins of others? Why or why not?
- ~~What songs or hymns are most effective in helping you connect with God?~~
- ~~What does it mean that human beings are created in "God's likeness" (v. 9)?~~
- How do you interpret James's use of rhetorical questions in verses 11 and 12?

FINALIZE YOUR LIST OF QUESTIONS

Here's an important piece of advice: don't incorporate too many questions into your final plan. A good rule of thumb is to write from five to ten questions for every hour your group will spend in discussion. That may not seem like enough, but think about it. Answering ten questions in a period of an hour means each question would receive only six minutes of attention from the entire group.

It's much better to explore the most important questions deeply than to take a shotgun approach and try to cover a whole spread of questions in a shallow way.

After the preceding steps, you should have several questions that will work well in your upcoming group meeting. The final step is to pick out the ones you believe have the most potential for sparking and maintaining a meaningful discussion.

To cut down your list of questions, start by making sure no

"discussion-killers" remain. If you find some, try to find a way to rewrite or edit them so they can be more effective. If they're just bad questions, let them go. If you still have too many questions, make a judgment call—which questions will be most helpful for your specific group?

Here's the final list of questions I prepared for my group meeting on James 3:1–12:

> ➤ What did you find surprising or significant or confusing about these verses?
> ➤ What are the primary images James uses in this passage, and what do they communicate?
> ➤ As you are comfortable, talk about moments from your past that support James's claim in verse 8: "[The tongue] is a restless evil, full of deadly poison."
> ➤ In what ways can the tongue be used for good?
> ➤ In which of these verses (if any) do you believe James is speaking hyperbolically?
> ➤ How much control can a human being gain over their tongue this side of eternity?
> ➤ What steps can we take to minimize the damage caused by the tongue within this group?

Before I move on to the topic of incorporating worship and prayer in a group meeting, let me mention one last thing: this process of crafting great discussion questions for your group does not have to be time-consuming, complicated, or difficult. In fact, it can become second nature given a little practice and concentration.

As you think deeply about the discussion questions you present to your group, you will more easily recognize those that boost or kill conversations. And the more you go through the process of writing discussion questions, working with stress points, and winnowing out the best material, the easier that process will become.

Chapter 9

Planning for Worship and Prayer

It's happened dozens of times during my tenure as a small group leader. I'm in the middle of facilitating a spirited discussion when I glance at the clock and, with a jolt, realize I should have dismissed the group ten minutes ago.

It's not that going ten minutes over the allotted time is a big deal. Rather, what causes that jolt is the realization that I still have elements I want the group to experience—more of the essential activities I'd planned on incorporating into the meeting.

For me, the essential activities that most often get left behind are worship and prayer. And judging by the emails I've received over the years, I'm not the only one who experiences this on a regular basis. Indeed, many group leaders have asked me how they can manage time within their group meetings so worship and prayer don't get left behind. And I've received many more emails from small group pastors who want advice on how to make worship and prayer a greater priority for their group leaders.

Fortunately, group leaders can take two steps to avoid regularly neglecting worship and prayer in their group meetings.

First, don't wait until the end of each group meeting to engage in worship and prayer. Maybe that sounds obvious, but I've drifted into a rut many times when it comes to how I structure each gathering. And it doesn't help that most prewritten Bible studies follow a predictable pattern: icebreaker, discussion, an application question, then worship and prayer.

I recommend shaking things up as you prepare for your group meetings over time. It's a great idea to start a meeting with prayer, for example. Or to lead a worship activity in the middle of a series of discussion questions. Or to spend an entire group meeting in worship and prayer every now and then.

Second, don't settle for a generic view of worship and prayer. Worship can be more than breaking out a guitar and singing a few songs. Prayer should include more than going around the circle and taking requests. When you plan worship and prayer activities that are more robust and diversified, your group members will respond in a more positive way—and you'll have an easier time featuring those activities in your group meetings.

With that in mind, here are several strategies that can help you make full-bodied plans for worship and prayer within your group meetings.

Planning for Worship

My son Daniel was a huge fan of the movie *How to Train Your Dragon* during his younger years, and he was delighted to receive a miniature Night Fury dragon as a Christmas gift. If you haven't seen that film, picture a sleek, jet-black reptile with the wings of a bat and the eyes of a crocodile. (Yeah, it's a pretty cool toy.)

The neat thing is that Daniel's Night Fury is an exact replica of the dragon from the movie—it has all the same markings and features, just condensed into a package that's smaller and safer.

Keep that image in mind, because I'm afraid that's what many of us attempt to do with worship in our groups—create a miniature replica of Sunday mornings that's smaller and safer.

It's an easy temptation to embrace, because so many people enjoy the thrill of worship on Sunday mornings. We like being carried away by musical instruments and a sea of voices all praising God in unison. We also like the convenience of a PowerPoint display all queued up to lead us through the verses and repeating choruses. So when it comes time to worship in our groups, we try to imitate that kind of atmosphere. But more often than not we end up robbing our worship experiences of their power.

The problem, of course, is that the worship setting in a group is much different from what happens on Sunday mornings. There is no band. No staff member or layperson spending hours in preparation for the worship set. No PowerPoint slides or specially produced videos.

And that's okay. Your group is an intimate gathering where a few people can assemble and seek to encounter God together. It's a different atmosphere for worship, not better or worse. Jesus said, "Where two or three gather in my name, there am I with them" (Matt. 18:20), not "Whenever everyone gets together on Sunday morning."

That being the case, here are several activities and practices that can help you embrace the intimacy of group worship:

Prayer early and often. The purpose of worship is to connect with and praise God in a deep, meaningful way. And nothing facilitates that kind of experience like prayer— especially when a group of Christians focus on seeking the Lord in unison.

Readings. Prewritten readings based on Scripture can be powerful as a group worship activity. Give people a chance to read God's Word out loud, and be sure to include moments of silence that allow those words to soak in. You can also find several books containing prayers and exhortations to

God (similar to the psalms), most of which are a great way to express worship and devotion. One time-tested example is *The Book of Common Prayer.*

Object lessons. Consider leading a worship activity based on a concrete image or object lesson. Have group members hold lit candles in a darkened room, for example, or ask them to write some of their fears on slips of paper and then nail them to a wooden cross. These activities often help people experience an abstract concept in a new and more emotive way.

Communion. Jesus instituted the practice of Communion during a dinner with twelve of his closest friends. Referring to that event, Paul gave these instructions to Jesus's followers: "*Whenever* you eat this bread and drink this cup, you proclaim the Lord's death until he comes" (1 Cor. 11:26; emphasis added). That gives you a great opportunity to worshipfully lead your group members in a time of remembering Christ's sacrifice and resurrection.

It should be noted that some church and denominational leaders may not look favorably on a small group practicing Communion. If that's the case in your church culture, you probably don't want to make waves over the issue. Your group can worship in other ways, after all.

Singing! I certainly don't want to imply that singing isn't an appropriate form of worship for a small group. It is, and singing together as a group can be powerful. But singing shouldn't be your group's only form of worship, and doing so should be tailored for a group setting. Give an opportunity for requests, for example. Or let different people take the lead from song to song.

Remember, embrace worship in your group as a chance to connect with God—and with the other members of your group—in an intimate setting.

Planning for Prayer

The most frustrated I've ever felt in a group meeting was during a prayer time several years ago. It started badly when we "went around the circle" to share requests. Every person seemed to share at least one completely tangential concern—their uncle's neighbor was thinking about a career change or someone at work had done something silly and offended other people.

When the time came to actually start praying, I made a big mistake. "I'll open us in prayer," I said. "Who's willing to close?" I heard only silence for at least thirty seconds—complete with people awkwardly looking at the ceiling or their own toes—and I mentally kicked myself for even asking the question. Finally, mercifully, my wife volunteered to close, and we got rolling.

I was already feeling distracted at this point, so my opening salvo was pretty generic: "Lord, we're thankful that You've helped us gather here safely tonight. Please bless us as we bring our requests to You." Other group members continued in that vein—regurgitating different requests and sometimes throwing in bits of advice for good measure.

One guy in particular got my blood boiling. He prayed for several minutes straight and kept tossing around clichés and jargon phrases like rice at a wedding. I remember thinking, *Somebody needs to teach this guy how to pray.*

Then it hit me: that somebody was me. I was the one charged with teaching this guy how to pray. In fact, I was charged with leading the whole group in meaningful, productive times of prayer.

And I had failed.

In recent years I've learned several strategies for facilitating a fruitful prayer experience during a group meeting (and I share many of those strategies in chapter 12). But I've also determined that group leaders need to take an important step of preparation *before* each group meeting. Specifically, they need to plan diverse prayer experiences that will be meaningful within the context of each group meeting. In other words, we need to put some time and effort into thinking about how to pray differently for different group meetings. It's okay to "go around the circle" with prayer requests every now and then, but if that's the only method we use for group prayer, the group will be in danger of falling into a rut.

So here are several ideas for prayer activities that can be tailored to your group as you prepare for specific group meetings:

Concert prayer. This technique is as simple as it is revolutionary. Everyone around the circle talks about their prayer requests, and then everyone prays for those requests together. Out loud. At the same time. Your group literally becomes a symphony of prayer as everyone lifts their voices and supplications in unison.

Having tried this in several groups, I can say that your group members may feel a little self-conscious at first—maybe even a little uncomfortable. But trust me when I say they'll start to see the benefits after a few repetitions. The unity your group will experience through this chorus of prayer is wonderful, and people will no longer be worried about saying something silly, because nobody else is listening.

Immediate prayer. With this technique, the group prays for each person immediately after they share their prayer requests and areas of praise. For example, if Rob notes three concerns or praises he'd like the group to pray about, everyone stops right there and prays for each of Rob's requests. Then the same thing happens with the next person and the next and the next. (It's not important for every single group member to pray for every single request; people can pray as they feel led.)

This way group members don't have to sift through all the requests for the entire group when it comes time to actually pray. You don't have to worry about remembering everything, so you can concentrate on praying and agreeing with others who pray. (As a side note, the group can pray in a "normal" fashion for each person's requests, or it can use the concert prayer method.)

Subgrouping for prayer. This is a variation of the two previous techniques, where the group divides into three or four subgroups in order to facilitate the process of prayer. The idea is to make it easier for group members to concentrate on each other and on the process of praying without feeling the weight of being responsible for the entire group at all times.

Themed prayer. The idea here is to pick a theme on which your group will concentrate its prayers for a particular session. Options for themes include troubles or blessings your group members are experiencing at work, fears people are struggling with, and family prayers and praises.

Segmented prayer. You may have heard someone break prayer down into four different components: adoration, confession, thanksgiving, and supplication. This is often referred to in acronym form as the ACTS of prayer or a prayer CAST. In segmented prayer, a group focuses on one of these components for an individual group meeting. So this method is similar to "themed prayer," except the group focuses on a specific aspect of prayer rather than on a theme of prayer requests.

Of course, these are not the only activities you can consider as you prepare to lead others in prayer. Read, explore, experiment, and build a system of prayer that's best suited for your group.

Remember the Big Idea

As with icebreakers, it's common for prayer and worship to be viewed as separate from the learning activities within a group meeting. A group may engage in discussion and application around a specific theme, but that theme is dropped when the time comes for prayer or worship at the end of a meeting. This way of thinking has been echoed by several small group leaders I've spoken with, and it's prevalent in many of the prewritten Bible studies available.

But such a separation is unnatural. If the primary goal of a group meeting is spiritual growth and transformation, then participants need to do more than engage in discussion around the truths found in God's Word. They need opportunities to respond to those truths. And worship and prayer are great ways to help your group members begin such a response.

So here is my advice: as often as you can, make a connection between the activities you choose for prayer and worship and the big idea of your group meeting. You can make connections with specific verses or themes explored in the group meeting that fall under the umbrella of the big idea.

Continuing the case study on James 3:1–12, remember my big idea: *the words we speak can accomplish powerful things for good and evil.*

Several worship activities would have fit well with this theme— the most obvious being to invite us all to use our tongues for good by singing songs of praise or maybe reading through the lyrics together. I also could have found a responsive reading that addresses the power of the tongue. Or I could have taken a different route and led the group in a time of silent contemplation and worship. (It would have been fun to pass out tongue depressors for such an experience as an object lesson.)

In the end, I chose to lead the group in reading Psalm 145 out loud, which ends with this verse: "My mouth will speak in praise of the Lord. Let every creature praise his holy name for ever and ever" (v. 21).

Leading a time of concert prayer would have been a great choice for a prayer activity to fit my big idea for James 3:1–12. I could have also divided the group into smaller clusters and asked each subgroup to pray through a different psalm.

But I decided to try a segmented prayer, where we focused on the confession of sin. Specifically, I asked the group to consider confessing times when their speech had hurt another person or misrepresented what a follower of God should be. It was a somber experience, but beneficial—and a great way to respond to James's admonition that using our tongues for evil "should not be."

Chapter 10

Finalizing Curriculum

I'm not a fan of male stereotypes in general, but one in particular gets me fired up: the idea that men don't ask for directions. I get irritated whenever I hear that because I'm positively a man, and I'm also a big fan of asking for directions. Whether it's gas station attendants or people walking their dogs, if I'm lost, I find somebody who can get me back on the right track.

Really, I like to carry directions with me so I don't get lost in the first place. In fact, before the GPS revolution, it was common for me to put together folders for our family road trips—complete with detailed printed sheets for driving directions, hotel information, landmarks, and more.

It's important for group leaders to take a similar approach with their group meetings. And that's where a teaching plan comes in handy.

The word *curriculum* carries different meanings for different people. But in the context of a small group, it really just means a plan for the different activities a group will experience in the short-term (a single group meeting) and long-term (like a six-week curriculum on the book of James). Incidentally, many group practitioners have started referring to the activities within a single gathering as an "agenda" or "meeting plan," which is a helpful distinction and one I use at times throughout this chapter.

So your final step in preparing for a group meeting should be putting together a finished plan that helps you navigate the different activities you want to experience with your group. That's true whether you're using a prewritten curriculum or have come up with everything yourself.

Finalizing Prewritten Curriculum

My wife is an excellent cook, and she prefers to make all her preparations from scratch when she can. But with several children running around the house, she's been forced to take a few shortcuts now and then.

For example, one of my favorite meals is a mandarin orange chicken that she buys from Trader Joe's. The chicken is frozen, and Jess heats it in the oven for eighteen minutes. While it's cooking, she defrosts the two packets of sauce that are included and cooks up a cup of basmati rice. After she pulls the chicken out of the oven, she stirs in the sauce and puts everything back for another two minutes. Then she throws it on a plate with the rice and dribbles some extra sauce over the top. Next comes a really nice salad with spring greens, baby spinach, walnuts, dried cherries, sunflower seeds and some balsamic vinaigrette. The last touch is a cold glass of reverse-osmosis-filtered water.

Voila! She puts it all on the table while I gather the children, and we all have a great experience.

Keep that image in mind over the next few pages, because it's a useful picture as you think about using prewritten Bible studies in your group. They're great tools with the potential to spiritually nourish you and the other members of your community. But like that mandarin orange chicken, you never want to experience them straight out of the bag.

Fortunately, customizing a prewritten Bible study to fit the needs of your group takes only two steps: (1) cut any material that doesn't fit with your big idea, and (2) add supplemental material if necessary.

The Big Idea and Cutting Material

It's just as important for you to identify a big idea when using a prewritten study as it is when you develop a study from scratch. That's because a big idea is the best tool at your disposal for getting rid of unnecessary material.

Do you know that plastic octagonal toy just about every household in America with kids has owned at one point or another? The one with a different shaped cutout on each side? Toddlers have a blast sliding a three-dimensional triangle or oval or star through the correct cutout and then dumping all the shapes they just pushed inside back on the floor. Well, that's a great image for how the big idea works as you finalize your agenda for a group meeting.

When you identify a big idea for a particular study, it's like you're choosing a shape on that toy. Let's say a triangle for the purposes of this illustration. Then from that moment on, you'll get rid of anything in the study that doesn't fit through the triangle-shaped hole— anything that doesn't fit smoothly and easily into your big idea.

Maybe you feel uncomfortable with the idea of messing with a published Bible study. Maybe you don't feel confident in your ability to make the right decisions, or maybe you feel like you should stick with what the expert planned.

Well, I've written a good deal of curriculum in recent years, and I've edited quite a bit more. So hear me when I say this: just about every piece of prewritten curriculum you will ever download or purchase has way too much material for your group to cover. Way too much. And that's on purpose.

Those of us who produce and publish Bible studies have to think broadly. We're trying to include as much good material in each study as we can, because we don't know which specific elements will be useful to a given group or class. In other words, we're counting on you to use what's helpful for your group, and we're counting on you to discard the rest.

With that in mind, here are guidelines for cutting at least three types of material within an existing study:

Entire sections. Don't feel shy about cutting away entire sections of a Bible study. If the curriculum you're using contains four teaching points and only two of them apply to your big idea, be ruthless. Cut the study in half and focus on the material that fits smoothly with your big idea.

You can also use your group members' knowledge and experience to filter out unnecessary material. For example, say one of the teaching points in your study is designed to explain the meaning of sanctification, but you know your group members are already familiar with that doctrine. Feel free to skip that section or to ask a quick review question and then move on. (The same is true if some of the material in the study conflicts with the beliefs of your group or church.)

Discussion questions. First, make sure to cut out any discussion-killing questions you find in a prewritten study. Yes, those questions exist in published material. And yes, they still need to go.

Next, one of the most common mistakes I see group leaders make is trying to get through all the discussion questions included in a Bible study. As in the group meeting is halfway over and its members have addressed only a quarter of the questions, so the leaders try to hurry people along in the name of "keeping things moving."

That's a big mistake, because few things shut down the activity of the Holy Spirit more than a group leader scurrying to get everything done. Plus, it makes for lousy conversation and keeps discussion at the surface.

The best way to combat this bad habit is to go through the discussion questions before your group meeting and cross out the ones you don't think have as much application to your people. Just cross them out. This will help you focus on the questions most pertinent to your group. (And if you get through all those questions, you can always go back and use the ones you crossed out.)

Activities. Many prewritten Bible studies don't include icebreakers or additional activities for worship, prayer, or application. If you come across a study that contains that kind of material, count yourself lucky. At the same time, don't feel like you have to use canned activities if they're generic or don't fit what you want to accomplish in a group meeting. You may need to think of something new, and that's okay.

A note about participant's guides: Your curriculum may include journals or guides or workbooks for the other participants in your group. If so, don't worry about explaining what material you've cut out or the changes you've made. Just give clear directions as you guide everyone during the group meeting. ("We're going to start with an activity that's not in your workbook," or "Let's skip down to question five.")

Last, be ruthless when you preview and prepare your material each week. Yes, you may be cutting out good material. You may be cutting out interesting and useful material. But that's okay, because your goal is to include the best material.

Adding Material (If Necessary)

Once you've cut everything that doesn't connect with the big idea for a group meeting, take an objective look at what's left. Does enough material remain to cover what you want to accomplish?

Here are some time factors to keep in mind as you make that decision:

> For an hour of group discussion, you'll need 5 to 10 quality discussion questions.
> Icebreakers and learning activities typically last from 2 to 10 minutes.
> A group worship experience will require 15 to 30 minutes.
> I recommend setting aside 15 to 30 minutes for a quality prayer experience.
> I recommend providing at least 15 minutes of hangout time for each group meeting. This can happen before or after the official group schedule if time is tight.

You also need to ask yourself another set of questions before putting the final stamp of approval on a prewritten Bible study:

> Is the material diverse enough to provide a well-rounded experience?
> Will it address different learning styles?
> Will the discussion questions help people engage on at least a few levels?
> Will you have an opportunity to discuss or practice application?

If you answer no to any of these questions, or if you don't have enough material, you'll need to do some extra work in order to prepare a full-bodied group meeting. This doesn't have to be overly complicated or strenuous. Use the strategies from chapters 6 through 9 to supplement whatever material you need—just like you were writing an activity or some discussion questions from scratch—and then move on.

Finalizing Your Own Curriculum

There are lots of reasons why group leaders choose to write their own curriculum. Some do it to save money. Others do it out of necessity when they can't find the right material. And still others do it simply because they enjoy the process.

Whatever reason applies to you, it's important that you make a commitment to produce something worthwhile. Because writing your own curriculum won't benefit your group if you don't know what you're doing or if you choose to cut corners. That's why the preceding chapters in this Part Two provide detailed instructions for planning the various activities within a group meeting—like icebreakers, learning activities, discussion questions, worship, and prayer—all relating to a big idea that keeps the group's purpose in focus.

The final step in the process is to organize everything into a plan that's easy to follow once the group meeting gets rolling. Preferably, this should be a plan that fits how you prefer to operate as a leader rather than your emulating what you've always seen in prewritten curriculum.

For example, I'm a read/write learner who prefers to organize information through words and lists. So when I put together an agenda for a group meeting, I usually create an outline.

The following plan is what I developed for the group meeting on James 3:1–12, including a few notes in brackets:

Scripture: JAMES 3:1–12

Big Idea: The words we speak can accomplish powerful things for good and evil. [I've found that writing out the big idea in this way helps me keep everything we do focused.]

Icebreaker [10 minutes]: Powerful words. [When I think of an icebreaker or learning activity, I usually don't write the whole experience out word-for-word. But I do jot down several notes to myself so I'll remember what to do.]

- Bring magazines. Bring scissors, construction paper, and glue for a collage.
- Have group members hunt for powerful words (5 minutes).
- Let people share what they found.
- Cut out and glue to make a collage.

Unpacking questions [5 minutes]:

- Which words found by other group members did you find to be especially powerful? Why?
- From what source do you most often encounter powerful words?

Read James 3:1–12 out loud. Discussion questions [30 minutes]:

- What did you find surprising or significant or confusing about these verses?
- What are the primary images James uses in this passage, and how do you react to them?
- As you are comfortable, talk about moments from your past that support James's claim in verse 8: "[The tongue] is a restless evil, full of deadly poison."
- In what ways can the tongue be used for good?
- In which of these verses (if any) do you believe James is speaking hyperbolically?
- How much control can a human being gain over their tongue this side of eternity?
- What steps can we take to minimize the damage caused by the tongue within this group? (application)

> **Worship [5 minutes]:** Collective reading of Psalm 145.
> (Does anyone want to respond?)
>
> **Prayer [10 minutes]:** Opportunity to confess sin as it
> relates to our speech.

Again, this is the method of organization I find most efficient and helpful when I prepare for a group meeting. You may not be interested in creating an outline, and that's okay. But I do recommend you create some version of a plan prior to your gathering.

If you're more of a visual person, you might get better results from arranging the material into boxes or some kind of chart. If you have an auditory learning style, you may want to spend time talking through the lesson plan with a friend and just jot down a few basic notes.

Find a system that works for you both during your preparation time and the actual group meeting.

Beware the Dangers of Unintended Curriculum

Before closing this section on preparing for a group meeting, I need to address a hidden danger that afflicts many groups: unintended curriculum.

My wife and I were on vacation in Southern California when we decided to visit San Juan Capistrano Mission, an adobe chapel complex founded by Father Junipero Serra in 1776. In the back of the mission was a small replica of the gardens that produced much of the monks' food for hundreds of years.

As we walked through the garden, I noticed a particularly leafy bush with several green lizards lounging among its branches. A large sign in front of the bush read "Please don't chase or catch our lizards. They lose their tails if you grab them."

Well, you can probably guess the first thought that went through my mind: *I would like to see a lizard's tail fall off.* If I hadn't been with my wife and our young (impressionable) children, I'm sure I would have reached out and grabbed a lizard just to see what would happen next.

Thus the danger of unintended curriculum.

UNDERSTAND THE DANGER

As we group leaders prepare to lead a Bible study, we generally approach each meeting with a certain goal in mind. We have specific principles we'd like to explore with our group members—truths we hope they'll understand better after our lesson.

That is our intended curriculum. It's what we've outlined in the big idea. It's what we want to communicate.

For example, consider a group leader who's structured a discussion around John 3:16: "For God so loved the world that he gave his one and only Son, that whoever believes in him shall not perish but have eternal life." Her intended curriculum would likely include the biblical principles of atonement and redemption.

If, however, that leader were to continually stress the idea that Christians "shall not perish but have eternal life" without providing a context or explanation for that terminology, it's possible that a new Christian in the group could come away with the idea that Christians don't experience physical death.

That would be an example of unintended curriculum.

This situation describes the most common form of unintended curriculum—a false belief transferred through ignorance about a particular text, or ignorance about proper methods for leading a discussion. In other words, unintended curriculum can pop up if a group leader does a poor job of either interpreting or communicating a passage of Scripture.

But other unintended curriculum can occur, including the following:

An ill-considered environment. The physical or emotional environment of a group meeting can itself become a kind of curriculum. If group members sit in two rows facing the leader, for example, whatever that leader says will come with an air of authority. When the group sits in a circle, the environment is based more on equality of thought.

Unbalanced priorities. What we continually emphasize as group leaders says a lot about what we consider valuable—and not valuable. Therefore, our choice of topics can be an influential source of unintended curriculum. For example, consider a youth leader who spends forty weeks out of a year discussing sexual purity but only four weeks discussing salvation. He could very easily send a message that God is more interested in restricting our behavior than developing a personal relationship with us.

Personal bias. In a similar way, a leader's opinions on specific subjects can produce unintended curriculum. Think of a group leader railing against the evils of Darwinian evolution. If she chooses to attack the scientists and scientific principles in support of evolution, she can easily impress her group members with the idea that all science is inherently at war with the Bible.

Much of the unintended curriculum that is covertly dished out in small groups is relatively harmless. Theological misinterpretations can be easily corrected by asking questions. Personal biases are regularly overcome through exposure to a variety of opinions and other sources.

But sometimes unintended curriculum can have devastating and even deadly consequences. This happens when a group leader (or a group member) unintentionally communicates something false about the nature of Christianity itself.

Boredom is probably the most common example of unintended

curriculum. Put simply, when a group leader turns the truths of God's Word into a series of boring questions or activities, they do more than passively fail to deliver their intended curriculum. They actively teach the group that the Bible itself is boring. And after continued exposure to such unintended curriculum, the members of that group may conclude that the experience of Christianity as a whole is also boring and thus not worth pursuing.

Ouch!

The same is true when we fail to help others see how biblical truths can be applied to everyday life. Or when our personal lives and decisions directly contradict what we've taught or communicated in the group. Or when the tenor of a group discussion is caustic and offensive.

Unintended curriculum can also pop up in how we manage the personal dynamics of our groups and classes. As an example, think back to the most annoying person you've ever encountered in a group meeting. Now determine what was the most annoying or disruptive behavior that person indulged in. Maybe he tried to answer every question and always talked way too much. Maybe she was judgmental and routinely put down other members of the group. Maybe he fell asleep all the time.

Whatever the behavior was, the response of the group leader (and the group as a whole) taught something to that individual—and to the rest of the group. If the behavior was ignored or left unaddressed, that implied the negative behavior was acceptable. Chances are that the behavior continued until the group either learned to live with it, disbanded, or eventually asked the person to leave. This obviously was not the intention of the leader or the group—it was unintended curriculum.

WHAT YOU CAN DO ABOUT IT

My goal in pointing out the nature and reality of unintended curriculum is not to make you paranoid as a group leader. I don't think it would be profitable for us all to spend hours examining and reexamining our discussion questions and learning activities in search of any train of thought that could potentially be boring or offensive. But I would like us as group leaders to take a step back every now and then and try to examine the groups we lead from the perspective of those who experience them. Better yet, I would like us to solicit feedback from our group members. What sticks out to them during group meetings? What have they learned in recent weeks? What did they like? What did they dislike? Were they offended by anything said? Were they excited?

Taking the time to evaluate ourselves and the experience of our groups will do wonders to ensure that people are experiencing what we intend them to experience—and nothing more.

PART 3

Hitting the Trail

Back when I played football, my week of athletics was divided into two types of events: practice and the game.

Interestingly, the activities I participated in were similar for both events. I spent most of my time running around, pushing other large men, running some more, and tackling smaller men. But my frame of mind was drastically different from one to the other. Playing in a game carried a much higher level of intensity—and much greater consequences if I made a mistake.

I feel the same way about the difference between preparing for the activities in a group meeting and actually leading people through those activities. Preparation and execution are both important factors in creating an atmosphere conducive to spiritual growth. But everything seems more significant when other people are around.

I've written Part Three of this book to help small group leaders feel more confident and equipped to manage the intensity of a group meeting:

> Chapter 11 provides direction for leading the discussion portion of a group meeting.
> Chapter 12 outlines tips and strategies for leading other elements, including fellowship, learning activities, prayer, worship, and more.
> Chapter 13 is a troubleshooting guide for some of the common problems that can surface during group gatherings or classes.
> Chapter 14 explores application on a deeper level and offers inspiration for your important role as a group leader.

Chapter 11

The Art of Leading
Group Discussions

Do you think it's easy or hard to learn how to drive?

I like to put myself in the shoes of a fifteen-year-old boy when I think about that question. On the one hand, the act of driving itself seems pretty easy. The kid has watched his parents do it for as long as he's been alive, after all, and it must seem to him like the whole experience involves nothing more than pushing a couple of pedals and turning a wheel.

Yet imagine that kid's surprise when someone shows him that thick packet of information people are supposed to study before they take the written test for a driver's license. Or the first time he tries to parallel park. Or the first time he approaches a four-way stop sign without anyone in the car to remind him who has the right-of-way.

Our fictional kid learns pretty quickly that becoming proficient in the skill of driving won't happen until he achieves mastery over several subsets of abilities, attitudes, and rules.

Leading a group discussion for the first time is a similar experience. Like driving, the basic idea is pretty simple: the group leader asks a question, waits for a few people to answer, and then asks another question. Repeat until the allotted forty-five minutes are over. Right?

But those of us who have led group discussions for years understand that so much more is involved. Skills need to be learned and developed, habits need to be formed, principles need to be applied, and more.

That's the focus of this chapter.

Context: Laying the Groundwork

At the beginning of this book, I mentioned that many small group leaders feel the need to teach their group members by providing a lot of information, principles, and theories instead of leading an actual discussion. In case there's any ambiguity, let me be clear: this is a bad idea. It's called lecturing, and it should be reserved for professors behind their lecterns (and to some extent pastors behind their pulpits).

But that doesn't mean group leaders should have nothing to say. We should. In fact, I believe it's important for us to spend a little bit of time explaining the context of a Bible passage or topic before the group digs into a discussion.

I also believe group leaders need to address context on two levels: textual and personal.

TEXTUAL CONTEXT

The textual context of a Bible passage is the frame that surrounds it and gives it meaning. This frame is made up of several elements:

> - The verses that come immediately before and immediately after the Scripture passage under discussion
> - The book of the Bible that contains the passage under discussion
> - All passages of Scripture that were written by the author of the passage under discussion

> The Bible as a whole
> The culture and historical setting experienced by the author as he wrote the passage under discussion

The first two elements are often referred to as the "immediate context." They operate like the white lines on both sides of a road—they show us where the text has come from and where it's going, and they provide a boundary that keeps us from wandering away from the text's proper meaning. The final three elements are often referred to as the "broad context." They operate like a map, showing us the country surrounding that particular road on all sides.

Here's my point: one of your jobs as a group leader is to provide a brief overview of the textual context for the verses your group will be interacting with during a discussion. And you want to provide that overview before the discussion gets started.

You don't want to get carried away, of course. You don't have to dig through a myriad of commentaries and hit your group members with every piece of relevant information you uncover. That would be lecturing, and lecturing is bad.

No, your goal is simply to highlight a few facts and ideas that wouldn't be considered "common knowledge" and that you believe will be helpful to your group members during the discussion. Hopefully, that kind of information will be included with the curriculum your group is using. If not (or if you wrote your own material), you should be able to compile some useful information during the process of identifying a big idea, writing discussion questions, or developing another part of your study.

PERSONAL CONTEXT

Personal context refers to your group members' experiences and attitudes that frame their interaction with each passage of Scripture. In other words, just as the verses before and after a passage have an impact on its meaning, your group members' personal stories will impact how they interact with that passage and its meaning. This includes their stories as individuals as well as the collective story of the group as a whole.

To continue the analogy I started earlier, if the broad context of a Scripture passage is like a map, and the immediate context is a single road on that map, then the personal context is the condition of the person attempting to follow that road on that map.

That being the case, another of your jobs as a group leader is to maintain some level of awareness regarding the condition of your group members as they prepare to discuss a passage of Scripture.

If most of your group seems exhausted, for example, and you had planned on delving into a deep doctrinal exploration of Romans 5, you may need to change your plan a bit. Or if you were going to lead a discussion on a Scripture passage that deals with grief (Psalm 22, for example) but then you learn that one of your group members just experienced a death in their extended family, you have a responsibility to include their experience in the group's discussion of the text.

The bottom line is this: it's important for you as a leader to highlight the textual context of a Scripture passage in order to help your group explore that passage more fully. In the same way, it's important for you as a leader to point out anything from the lives of your people that may serve as an obstacle or an enhancement to the group's discussion.

AN EXAMPLE

My small group recently worked through the book of Revelation, and we started by exploring the letters to the seven churches in Revelation 2 and 3. Here are the nuggets of textual and personal context I provided for the group when we studied the letter to the church in Pergamum (Rev. 2:12–17):

> ➤ Reminder: all seven letters to the churches follow the same structure. They start with an image of Jesus; they talk about

what the church has done well; they talk about what the church has done wrong; they encourage the church to stand strong in the middle of hard times; and they describe a reward for those who do stand strong.

> Pergamum was located on the coast of the country we call Turkey today.

> Pergamum was one of the rare cities in the Roman Empire allowed to administer capital punishment, which was called "the right of the sword." This is important for understanding verses 12 and 16.

> I understand that several of you are excited to start digging into the juicy parts of Revelation that deal with the end of the world and all that. But that starts in chapter 4, so we'll need to stay away from those discussions until we get a little further into the text.

See the idea? Not too long. Not too much information. Just a few helpful facts and observations to prepare the group for an interesting discussion.

How to Facilitate a Fantastic Discussion

It's true that the basic structure of a group discussion is nothing more than a series of questions and answers between the leader and group members. But in the same vein, I could say that playing a guitar is nothing more than moving your hand across the strings, or that Olympic high diving is nothing more than falling into a pool.

In reality, several subtle skills and competencies enable discussion leaders to effectively manage the question-and-answer process in a meaningful way. Most group leaders develop these skills by experience—especially by making mistakes. I've listed some of the more important strategies here to help you maximize the former and avoid the latter.

WHY SILENCE IS YOUR FRIEND

The majority of group leaders I've encountered are uncomfortable with silence in their groups. They don't like it. They find it awkward and off-putting.

That's a natural reaction. We live in a noisy world, after all. Between televisions, phones, radios, and computers, something is always pumping sound in our direction—which means a moment of silence during a discussion time can be viewed as problematic. Unnatural.

Even more, group leaders often feel like they've made a mistake when they ask a question and receive only an extended period of silence in return. They think the question must have been bad or at least presented in a bad way. As a result, they develop a habit of responding to silence by answering the question themselves or moving on. (One reason this can happen is that group leaders feel insecure about their role or their ability to guide the conversation in the first place.)

Unfortunately, this habit is a deadly enemy of meaningful group discussion.

That's because silence during a group discussion is almost always a good thing—especially silence that occurs in response to a question. It means your group members are thinking. It means they're processing the question, comparing it to their understanding of the Scripture passage, integrating that with their own experiences, and deciding whether the result is something they want to share with the rest of the group.

All of that takes time.

In fact, it's common for people to spend thirty to sixty seconds processing a complicated question and deciding on a response. That may seem like an eternity to you as a group leader. (Go ahead and have a minute of silence right now to find out.) But that's because you've already been preparing for and thinking about the question for a significant amount of time. You already know what your answer would be.

Your group members, on the other hand, haven't been thinking about the question, which means they need time to do so during the group meeting. And that means you're going to encounter silence, so get used to it.

WHEN A QUESTION BOMBS

Having said that, sometimes you *will* ask a bad question or present a question in a bad way. Sometimes your group members will be silent not because they're thinking but because they have no idea how to respond to what you just asked.

You'll know when you've encountered one of these situations when the thirty to sixty seconds go by without anyone offering even a peep. You'll see your group members glancing questioningly at each other, or maybe a couple of people will raise their eyebrows, or shrug their shoulders, or frown in a mystified way. The point is the body language of your group members will provide more than enough clues to help you decide if they're thinking deeply or are deeply confused.

When you realize a question has bombed, you have two options:

1. **Rephrase and try again.** If you can think of a way to restate the question, go for it. Try to find a different way to ask the question, or try to approach the topic from a whole new angle.
2. **Let it go and move on.** If you rephrase the question and another thirty to sixty seconds go by without any clarification on the part of your group members, don't press the issue. Say something like, "I guess that's a question we can explore later," or, "That was a dud!" Then move on to something else.

One final tip: in most cases, you should resist the urge to answer your own question if nobody else in the group has responded. Also resist the urge to try to rephrase the question in a way that makes your intended answer obvious. The last thing you want to do is give your group members the impression that you're trying to herd them toward a specific idea but they're too dumb to follow.

Three Important Words Every Group Leader Should Know

One of the perilous things about serving as a group leader is that your group members will invariably look to you as an authority on every issue covered during a discussion. Whether or not you're qualified, you'll be seen as an expert on the Bible, theology, culture, human interaction, and everything in between. This is because you carry the title *leader*, and everyone knows it.

That being the case, group members will typically look in your direction if something needs to be decided. When a question about an obscure doctrine pops up, you'll be expected to know the answer. When somebody doesn't understand a concept or term, you'll be asked to explain. When an argument or controversy develops, you'll be asked to determine who's right and who's wrong.

These situations are common in every group or class. They happen to every group leader. Consequently, most group leaders quickly feel a great deal of pressure to perform. They feel like they should rise to the occasion and become the expert everyone expects—even if they're not qualified.

You need to resist this temptation at all costs for two reasons. First, if you "wing it" and provide some kind of expert opinion on an issue you aren't really sure about, there's a good chance you'll cause some damage. This damage can range from confusing your group members to false teaching to hurt feelings—all bad.

Second, when you step into the role of expert and give your opinion about an issue, it usually puts the brakes on any kind of meaningful discussion that might have developed around that issue. Because when the group accepts your words as authoritative, there's nothing left to talk about. This isn't always a terrible thing, but it does have the potential to squelch positive interaction between your group members, the text, and the Holy Spirit.

So when you don't feel confident about stepping into the role of expert, just use these three simple words: "I don't know." Be honest and allow the group to continue its exploration as a group. If the group continues to spin its wheels around a question or topic, you can add three more words: "I'll find out." This allows the group to move toward something new and gives you a chance to research and find an appropriate answer to share the next time the group gets together.

But what about when you do feel confident about sharing your opinion? What about those moments when you want to be the authority in order to answer a question or settle a dispute?

You have two options:

1. **Speak.** Being the group leader doesn't mean you never get to share your opinion or interact with the discussion. You're part of the group, you're part of the discussion, and if you have something to contribute, go for it. Just be aware that your contribution may end that particular branch of the discussion. So use discretion.

2. **Deflect.** If you're worried about becoming the "final answer," you always have the option of deflecting the discussion away from yourself and back to another member (or to the group as a whole). You can say, "I want to hear what Mike thinks about this topic," or "I'll share what I think in a minute, but I'd like to get some other opinions on the table first."

"Kill the Wabbits"

Tangential conversations—also known as "rabbit trails"—are another enemy of meaningful discussion. Of course, rabbit trails don't prevent people from talking or sharing their ideas. Rather, they whittle away the potential for spiritual impact as group members focus their attention on topics not relevant to the discussion.

Again, every group experiences rabbit trails. They're a natural by-product of human interaction and conversation. But it's your job as a leader to prevent your people from being distracted or harmed by them. That's what makes a leader a leader—the responsibility to keep the group focused. And, as in many cases, the best way to accomplish this is to simply be honest about your observations. Say something like, "I feel like we're getting off on a tangent here. Let's finish this conversation after the group meeting."

You're not being mean when you do this. You're not being authoritarian or acting like an ogre. You're fulfilling your role as a spiritual safari guide to keep your group members on the right path.

Maybe you're wondering, *How will I know if my group is wandering down a rabbit trail?* The answer is simple: remember your big idea. If the discussion starts moving away from the overarching theme you identified for that particular group meeting, you'll know it's time to pull the discussion back.

I'll address the looming shadow of personality issues in chapter 13, but now I want to tackle two common problems that specifically relate to discussion in a group meeting. I'm referring, of course, to people who talk too much or too little.

When a Group Member Talks Too Much

Here's a common refrain in the world of small groups today: few barriers can subvert the depth and transforming power of a group discussion faster than one or more group members dominating the conversation. And it's certainly true that some people can monopolize entire gatherings with their problems and perspectives, even to the point where they hinder the participation of everyone else in the group.

But I think some of us may need to calm down a bit on the issue of over-talkers in our groups. There are ways to manage those situations productively.

First, please be aware that some people naturally talk more than others. That's not necessarily a bad thing. So proceed with caution. For example, people with an auditory learning style usually process information by speaking out loud. It's just part of how they learn and how they remember facts or ideas they consider important. The same is often true of extroverts and social learners.

Before you label a group member as someone who talks too much, take a step back and try to look at the situation objectively. Are they really being disruptive and controlling, or do they just talk more than you would? Are they negatively affecting the group, or are you just annoyed as an individual?

In other words, is there really a problem? If your objective answer to that question is no, then you need to let it go. If your answer is yes, then by all means explore the following tips for handling group members who dominate a discussion.

BE ASSERTIVE

If you do encounter a genuinely dominating personality, the best solution is your own assertiveness as the group leader. Specifically, follow through on one of these three possibilities:

1. **Be assertive before the discussion.** If over-talking is a problem for your group, mention it in a broad way before you start a discussion. Tell the group you're looking for brief answers and thoughts. You may even consider setting a cap on the amount of time people are allowed to speak on each question—no more than one minute, for example. Also make it known that you want to hear from as many people as possible on each subject.

2. **Be assertive during the discussion.** If a group member ignores your request for brevity and begins to monopolize the

conversation, the best thing to do is nip it in the bud—even if that means interrupting them. Thank the person for their contribution, and then move the discussion in another direction by calling on another member or by asking a new question.

3. **Be assertive after the discussion.** If a person continually monopolizes the group's time, you may need to talk with them in private. State that you appreciate their willingness to contribute to the group's discussions, acknowledge and applaud the depth of their answers and opinions, but also be honest in sharing that the frequency and thoroughness of their responses can make it difficult for other group members to participate.

During these conversations it's possible to ask the dominant person for help in encouraging the rest of the group to talk, thus turning them into an ally.

MANAGE EYE CONTACT

Dominant personalities often associate eye contact from the discussion leader as a green light to talk. They may even interpret it as a request from you to share what's on their minds. Therefore, minimizing eye contact is an effective method for handling group members who talk too much.

To accomplish this without offending the person, invite them to sit next to you before the discussion begins. This will decrease the number of times you make direct eye contact with them, which should also decrease their tendency to talk.

MANAGE THE GROUP'S SILENCE

I mentioned earlier that many group leaders are uncomfortable with silence. Well, that can apply to group members as well. Sometimes members who feel awkward in times of silence will jump in and answer the question in an effort to end their discomfort. Therefore, by helping them get used to silence as a normal part of group life, you may decrease their need to talk over time.

One way to accomplish this is to ask group members to wait a specific amount of time before responding to a question. Say something like, "People need different amounts of time to process a discussion question and organize their thoughts for a response. To make sure everyone gets a chance to fully engage with our discussion, after I ask a question, I'd like everyone to wait twenty seconds before jumping in."

Of course, it's still possible that dominant group members will be the first people to speak once the waiting time period has expired. If that's the case, talk with them privately, using the steps previously outlined, and ask them to wait up to thirty seconds before speaking to make room for others to enter the conversation.

When Group Members Don't Talk Enough

At the opposite end of the spectrum are those group members who almost never say anything during a discussion. These folks can be especially unnerving to group leaders because they make us feel like we're not doing a good job of leading the discussion.

But again, we need to proceed with caution. Before you implement any of the following tips, take a time-out. Think objectively about the person in question and ask yourself, *Is this really a problem? Are they refusing to participate in the group, or do they just naturally talk less than others?*

If you still believe a problem exists, you can use several practical methods to help shy or quiet group members open up and get involved.

GIVE THEM TIME

First, make sure everyone has enough time to think. Again, silence is a friend, not an enemy. And if you aren't allowing all your group members enough time to adequately process a question and come up with a response, they won't be able to contribute.

In other words, be sure their silence isn't your fault.

MAKE EYE CONTACT

If a group member isn't contributing to the discussion, look directly at them as you ask the next question. Also be aware of the message being sent by your body language. Lean forward and smile as you ask the question. This reassures them you're interested in what they have to say.

If you're in a group where one or more people have a history of not participating in the discussion, use your choice of seating as an advantage. By sitting directly across from a quiet person, you maximize the amount of eye contact they'll receive from you.

BE ASSERTIVE

Many discussion leaders are hesitant to call on a specific group member for fear of intimidating or embarrassing them. But this can be a useful tool for group discussions where it's important for each person to participate. Asking a specific person to respond doesn't need to be authoritative or mean. Instead of demanding an answer, simply ask, "Steve, do you have anything to add?" or "Jamie, did anything strike you as especially interesting?"

When taking this route, be sure to accept "No" (or "I don't know" depending on the question) as an appropriate answer. Sometimes people genuinely don't have anything to add, or what they did plan to say was already mentioned by someone else.

Remember, as a discussion leader, it's not your role to drag information from each member of the group. Rather, it's your job to politely and assertively let each person know their opinions are valued and welcomed.

PRAISE, PRAISE, PRAISE

When a traditionally quiet person does speak out in the middle of a discussion, make sure it becomes a positive experience. Credit them for the thoughts expressed, and be assertive in inviting more by saying something like, "That's a great insight, Pat. We need to hear more from you in the future." Again, watch your body language, and be sure to smile. And if a quiet person says something you don't agree with or that doesn't quite align with the topic at hand, please don't grimace or even smirk. Instead, credit them for speaking out, then seek the opinion of another group member you trust to gently steer the conversation back on track.

Chapter 12

Leading Well-Rounded Group Meetings

I am very fond of well-made Italian cold-cut submarine sandwiches. In fact, if my diet was completely up to me, I'd probably eat Italian cold-cut subs for every meal—maybe with a glass of grape juice on the side. That way I'd be covered for each of the major food groups: grains, fruits, vegetables, meat, and mayonnaise.

Fortunately, my wife buys our food and makes the major decisions regarding what our family eats. That's why my body enjoys a healthy variety of fuels and is able to function properly (most of the time).

Some group leaders feel about discussion the same way I feel about Italian cold-cut subs, which means their gatherings are one-sided. But no matter how good or productive a group discussion may be, you need to add some variety to your gatherings—or else your group will become spiritually malnourished over time.

That variety includes the other key activities mentioned throughout the course of this book: social interaction, connecting with God's Word, learning activities, worship, and prayer. (It includes application, as well, but that's the subject of chapter 14.)

This chapter provides tips and strategies to help group leaders maximize those activities during a group meeting.

Social Interaction

In chapter 1, I mentioned that group leaders can't force people to grow spiritually. That job belongs to the Holy Spirit. It's also true that group leaders can't force people to connect relationally or enjoy each other's company.

What group leaders can do, though, is set up an atmosphere conducive to positive social interaction. In other words, you can provide people with a place to hang out and build relationships without a lot of distractions.

Here are some tips for doing just that.

If you have access to a thermostat, set the temperature at 67 degrees. That may sound cold to you, but trust me, the room will warm up plenty once all the bodies are there. Of course, if people are uncomfortable as the group meeting progresses, you can always make adjustments.

If possible, use lamps. Lamplight is easier on the eyes than overhead fluorescents are, and it creates a visually warm and inviting atmosphere.

Greet people as they arrive. Many people have a hard time injecting themselves into a conversation, and they'll remain on the sidelines for quite a while if nobody invites them to join in. The best thing you can do is make that invitation as soon as they walk in the door. "Mike and Katie, good to see you! We were just talking about the big picnic next week..."

Make sure everyone will have a proper seat. "We're glad you're here" and "There's a spot for you on the floor" are two statements that don't mesh.

Try to have participants sit on the same level. Many people don't like looking up or down in order to make eye contact and conversation with others. So to the best of your ability, have everyone sit at the same eye level; that is, try not to have some people sitting on chairs, others on the floor, and others standing.

Make food and drink available. Everyone likes a snack and something nice to drink. And those items help in creating a pleasant atmosphere. That doesn't mean you have to buy or prepare them every time, though. Once you've done what you can to set the stage for a relationally healthy atmosphere, your only other job is to jump in and enjoy some time with your group members.

Working with Teachable Moments

Every group that gathers for more than a few months eventually establishes some kind of routine—a rhythm of "doing life together." This is true on a macrolevel as group members see each other during meetings, see each other at church, meet together socially, interact online, or run into one another in stores or at sporting events. This is also true on a microlevel as the group establishes a regular pattern for its group meetings. Telling stories from the past week, discussing the Bible, eating food, sharing prayer requests—all these are shapes within that pattern.

This is natural. Your group members learn about one another as a by-product of these routines, and relationships become more solid. Your group members regularly encounter God's Word in the midst of these routines, and they grow both intellectually and spiritually.

The frustrating thing for us as group leaders is that these advances come slowly. They happen gradually, for the most part, and they happen below the surface. That means we don't always see a lot of fruit in the lives of our group members—we don't get many tangible signs that we're doing a good job leading them into life-changing encounters with each other and the Holy Spirit.

Sometimes, however, something happens in the group that breaks everyone free from these regular patterns—moments that pull the group away from its routine and into something different. This is when group members often experience a jump of some kind. Relationships solidify quickly into a deeper bond. Something clicks in a person's mind that enables them to truly understand and apply a doctrinal truth. Someone experiences conviction about an area of sin and confesses it openly.

I refer to these times as "teachable moments."

KEEP YOUR EYES OPEN

It's hard to write authoritatively about teachable moments because they're so difficult to pin down. They're spontaneous, unplanned bursts of insight or a sudden movement of the Holy Spirit.

Still, teachable moments do tend to fall into these broader categories:

Conflict. People are sinful, and when they gather enough times, a clash will eventually occur. This will happen in your group, but don't be afraid of it. When managed correctly (see chapter 13), conflict motivates people to open up about their feelings and experiences and speak truthfully. Indeed, a brief burst of conflict is often the spark that ignites a deep friendship.

Moments of extraordinary fun. Conflict isn't the only thing that solidifies relationships. When group members have a chance to really enjoy each other's company—on a camping trip, while sharing a hobby, or during an extended conversation—surprisingly powerful bonds can form.

Conviction of sin. Another area directed by the Holy Spirit is conviction of sin. Sometimes people feel convicted while discussing a Scripture passage, other times that happens while they verbalize a prayer request, and still other times it happens in a completely unexpected situation. But the end result is usually the same for the person experiencing conviction: an impulse to confess their sin and commit to repentance.

Of course, people don't always respond to this kind of conviction. Many fight it or hold off on taking action until they can speak with someone privately. Others don't respond verbally but show other signs of a deeper moment, like weeping, becoming unusually withdrawn, or looking confused.

Bursts of insight. As I mentioned earlier, sometimes group members are struck with a new understanding of a doctrine or biblical truth. All the pieces come together and they "get it." They not only understand what God is saying in His Word but how that truth applies to their lives—and how their lives will need to change because of it. Again, this is usually initiated by the Holy Spirit, and group members often respond by sharing what they've learned with the rest of the group.

Moments of crisis. Sometimes group members open up about a crisis they're experiencing. Maybe they lost a job, a loved one is seriously ill, or they're in financial peril. Sharing a personal experience of this magnitude takes extreme courage and vulnerability, which carries the potential for a powerful moment within the group.

As a group leader, one of your more important jobs is to keep an eye out for these kinds of teachable moments.

HOW TO RESPOND

Maybe you're wondering, *What am I supposed to do when our group experiences something like that?*

Good question. I generally have two guidelines when it comes to responding to teachable moments as a group leader:

Call a halt to the routine. When something powerful happens in your group, you as the leader must call attention to it. You cannot allow a potentially life-changing moment to be ground under the heels of routine.

Say something like, "Susan, I'm so grateful you were willing to share that with us. Let's take a pause right now and pray." Or "I know we have a lot of discussion questions to get through, but that was an amazing insight, Jim. Can we talk about that a little more?" Or even "Okay, I think some of us are feeling a little attacked right now. Let's all take a deep breath and start again."

Be ready to get out of the way. Once you've called the group's attention to a potential teachable moment, it's important that you don't try to maintain control over it. Teachable moments are not facilitated. They occur and grow organically, driven by either the Holy Spirit or the emotions and needs of your group members.

If some of this seems a little vague to you, I understand. Teachable moments are mysterious and profound events, and they defy a lot of step-by-step analysis. But they will happen, and they have the potential to make a significant impact in the growth of your group—if you're watching for and willing to embrace the mystery.

Leading Worship

Several variables are involved with leading worship in a group meeting—lots of activities to choose from and lots of ways to adapt those activities based on the makeup of your group. Keep in mind that I am not advocating a "paint by numbers" approach to worship in your groups. Variety is good, and you need to go with whatever works best for your people.

Still, I do want to mention some general guidelines you may find helpful as you lead your group members in times of worship.

For example, don't be afraid of silence during worship experiences. In fact, I highly recommend using silence as a key tool to enhance your times of worship. Just as people often need a little silence to consider a discussion question, they also reflect and contemplate more fully in quietness than when they're being directed to do something or say something. That means you can provide a richer experience of worship by using silence in the middle of Communion, before or after a Scripture reading, or in between songs.

Speaking of songs, keep the following in mind when you include music in your worship:

Have variety in the songs you choose. Some worship songs are snappy; some are somber. Some people like contemporary music; others like hymns. So when you pick out a set of songs for a particular group meeting (and I recommend three to five songs), try to incorporate some variety.

Put some thought into the order of the songs. Another benefit to having a diverse set of songs is that you can match the tone of the activities around your worship time. For example, if you worship after an icebreaker where the group was up and moving around, you should start with one or two peppy songs. Then you can finish with songs that have a slower tone, which will help your group transition to prayer or discussion. The same is true the other way around: if you worship after a time of prayer and contemplation, start with a song that's more somber.

Provide lyrics. You probably won't have hymnals or Power-Point slides in your group meeting, but you should still try to give people the words to the songs you choose. This doesn't have to be complicated—printing the lyrics on one or two sheets of paper is more than acceptable. You could also provide group members with a binder of lyric sheets and have them add new songs to it over the course of the group. (Do your best to obey copyright laws if you do start copying music.)

Here's one more thing to consider: maybe you shouldn't be leading worship at all. Maybe that role should be fulfilled by someone else within the group. Frankly, leading a group meeting is a draining experience—especially when you have to be "on" for the entire time. It's an act of offering yourself intellectually and emotionally in order to lead others.

For that reason, identifying one or more group members to take charge of worship can be a blessing in several ways. It provides you with a chance to recharge. It allows the worship leader to become more invested in the group through increased responsibility. And it helps the group experience more than one leadership style.

When you look for a volunteer to help with worship, don't assume it has to be someone who plays an instrument. That's a good place to start, but you should also keep your eyes open for the participants who become most engaged in your group's worship experiences. Do a person's eyes light up when you announce a Scripture reading or moment of contemplation? Does anyone display passion while singing a hymn? Has a group member already started taking the lead during some worship experiences?

If so, you've just identified a potential worship leader for your group.

Leading Prayer

I've read a lot of good material on the intersection of small groups and prayer, but none of it has been more helpful than Andrew Wheeler's book *Together in Prayer.* If you plan on praying during your group meetings, you need to read this book. Trust me.

Wheeler uses the metaphor of playing an instrument to describe the act of prayer. When we pray privately, we're soloists playing our music for God alone. But when we pray in a group, we're part of a symphony—a collection of individuals working together to lift a pleasing song toward our heavenly audience.

Unfortunately, the members of a typical small group aren't usually very good at working together. As Wheeler notes,

> Often . . . group prayer turns out to be more like a collection of soloists each playing their own piece than a concerted voice arising out of teamwork. One particularly experienced soloist plays a very long piece, and others are intimidated to follow. Multiple soloists each play a piece of their own, but there is no relationship between the pieces, no common refrain. The result is a cacophony of individual prayers and not true community prayer—not the picture Jesus had in mind in Matthew 18:19–20 when he spoke of two or more people coming together and agreeing in prayer.[1]

Does that sound like your group? If so, I'm afraid the problem boils down to a lack of leadership. People need to be taught how to work together in prayer; it doesn't come naturally. And as the group leader, you are the one to do the teaching. That's the bad news.

The good news is you only need to communicate two basic principles in order to begin solving the problem.

THE TWO DIMENSIONS OF GROUP PRAYER

Praying as a group involves two distinct dimensions: the vertical (our connection with God) and the horizontal (our connection with the other members of the group). Dissonance occurs when group members concentrate primarily on one dimension while ignoring the other.

For example, some people focus on the vertical dimension of prayer. They don't pay much attention when others are praying because they're planning what they'll say when it's their turn. When their turn comes, they sometimes deliver long, winding prayers that ignore the needs or preferences of those around them.

I think most people in small groups are the opposite, though. They get so caught up with the horizontal dimension that they fail to establish any kind of connection with God. This happens when group members feel pressure to sound impressive when they pray, resulting in a lot of jargon and clichés, or when they choose to lace their prayers with subtle hints and pieces of advice directed toward the people they're praying for. This is also reflected when a group member gets annoyed or frustrated by the way other people choose to pray; they focus on what others are doing wrong rather than participating in the prayer experience.

As a group leader, you need to help your group members understand these two dimensions of group prayer. Even more, you need to give them a vision of what prayer can be like when both dimensions are balanced—when the group is working as a team to create a single voice of adoration, thanksgiving, and supplication to God.

THE ROLE OF AGREEMENT IN GROUP PRAYER

Wheeler refers to this vision as "praying to God with people."[2] As each person prays out loud, their focus is primarily on God, not on the other group members. The prayers themselves are humble requests for God to intervene according to His will.

While one person is praying out loud, the other members of the group need to do more than passively listen to that person's words. They need to actively agree with the requests and praises being lifted up—to focus on supporting the person praying and echoing their words.

This kind of agreement takes different forms for different people. Some prefer to express their support in whispered words—"Yes,

Jesus" or "Please help him, Lord." Others prefer to remain silent and internally repeat the words being spoken. Still others focus on visual representations of the requests and praises offered by other members of the group.

The method of agreeing in prayer is not important, and group members should be encouraged to use whatever techniques come naturally to them and feel comfortable. What is important is that the people in your group actively engage in prayer even when they're not saying anything out loud.

PRACTICAL TIPS AND TRICKS

Here are some final bits of advice I'd like to offer before I close this section on group prayer.

Set boundaries for prayer requests. Maybe your group decides to mention only requests pertaining to people within the group and their immediate families. Maybe you ask group members to make no more than three requests each. Whatever you decide, a few reasonable boundaries need to be in place to ensure that group members don't feel like they're wasting their time listening to (and praying for) frivolous requests.

Provide pen and paper. Give your group members an opportunity to write down others' requests if they so choose. This is beneficial for prayer within the group, but it also gives everyone a chance to continue praying for the requests throughout the week.

Keep a prayer log. Speaking of keeping track, I highly recommend that your group appoint someone to keep a record of the requests prayed for and praises shared during your group meetings. The goal is twofold: to make sure requests are continually lifted up before God and to provide an official record of answered prayers so the group gets a picture of God's faithfulness over time.

One twist on this idea is to create a working cloud document or some other kind of accessible record for your group and their prayers. This probably should include a password so private prayers aren't made public.

Encourage various prayer postures. Kneeling helps some people adopt an attitude of submission and reverence during prayer; for others, kneeling just makes their knees hurt. When it's time to pray, encourage your group members to use whatever posture they feel comfortable with. Kneeling, standing, sitting, hands clasped, hands raised—whatever helps your group members connect with God and agree with the others.

Chapter 13

When a Group Meeting Doesn't Go as Planned

I go through a weird ritual whenever I purchase a new electronic gadget or gizmo. As soon as all the parts are put together or the item is installed, I pull out the instruction manual and read the troubleshooting section at the back. Doing so makes me familiar with everything that can go wrong, along with the different symptoms, so I'll know what to watch for if anything starts going haywire.

That's the basic idea behind this chapter.

While electronic gizmos are mass-produced, no two small groups are exactly the same. Each one is made up of unique individuals forming relationships and interacting with each other in unique ways. So it's impossible for someone like me to anticipate the specific malfunctions that may pop up in your group.

Still, a number of problems and confusing situations seem to be universal to a group setting. Some of them have been addressed in the earlier pages of this book (like over-talkers and under-talkers), but I want to examine a few of the most common scenarios here.

The malfunctions addressed in this chapter are issues I believe to be serious enough to warrant some expert assistance yet common enough that there's a good chance you'll be dealing with them at some point in your career as a group leader.

When Group Members Experience Strong Emotions

People are emotional beings. And while most of us prefer to keep most of our emotions in check most of the time, one of the signs of a healthy community is that participants become more and more comfortable sharing their feelings. It's a natural by-product of deepening relationships.

That being the case, it's likely you will encounter a burst of stronger-than-normal emotions at some point. Maybe a group member begins sobbing uncontrollably out of guilt, fear, or grief. Maybe someone vents a lot of angry words about a difficult or frustrating situation. Or maybe someone erupts in a shower of joy.

Whatever the case, it's important that you as the leader set the tone for how the group will respond to these strong emotions. Here are a few guidelines to keep in mind as you do.

Listen. Actively listen to the person expressing a strong emotion. Your first reaction may be to change the subject or find a way to help them calm down, but you must resist these temptations. Let the person speak, and make it clear to the group that you're listening.

Affirm. One of the best things you can do is name the emotion being expressed. "I hear you expressing a lot of [anger, grief, fear]." Validate the emotion instead of giving the impression that they "shouldn't feel that way."

Offer to help. When the initial venting of emotion subsides and you've been able to affirm what the group member is experiencing, give permission for them to seek help. "What can all of us do right now to help?" And make sure you include the entire group rather than attempting to manage all this by yourself. If the emotional member is close with someone else in the group, allow that person to offer comfort or a listening ear as needed.

Respond appropriately. If the group member is embarrassed and asks for a minute to regain control, allow them to do so. Offer the use of an empty room and ask if they would like to go alone or take a trusted friend. If the group member wants to talk—maybe to confess a sin, maybe to vent, maybe to seek advice—stop what the group was doing and listen.

Affirm again. When the situation has passed and the group member is returning to a more familiar state, make sure to affirm their willingness to share. "It takes a lot of courage to open up the way you did, and I want to thank you for trusting us with those feelings."

When Your Group Experiences Conflict

Not only are people emotional beings, but we're imperfect as well. We're sinful. And when imperfect, sinful, emotional people gather on a regular basis, they eventually clash.

We have to face it: conflict is an inevitable part of every group. Including yours.

But not all conflict is the same. In general terms, I like to break group conflict into two separate types: short-term and long-term.

SHORT-TERM CONFLICT

Sometimes conflict erupts spontaneously between group members. It can be the result of a flash-in-the pan reaction to something said, a debate that gets a little overheated, or just a group member having a really bad day.

Here are some basic guidelines to help you manage these small group solar flares.

Don't ignore issues. If you don't like getting in the middle of conflict (and few people do), your first instinct might be to ignore flare-ups between group members. That's a bad idea. Failing to address a negative behavior sends the message that such behaviors are acceptable to the rest of the group. This is especially true if one or more group members speaks in a way that is rude, offensive, overly sarcastic, or mean.

Your group won't remain a safe place for people if such behavior is tolerated and overlooked. Therefore, you need to step in when someone crosses the line.

At the same time, you may encounter a situation where your group responds appropriately to conflict or negative behavior without your leadership. That is more than okay! If your group has reached a place where participants point out negative behavior and address it on their own, your job is that much easier, and you can feel free to remain in the background until needed.

Address conflict quickly. Another bad habit group leaders often fall into is trying to address a flare-up after the group meeting has ended. They don't want to embarrass the people involved or make a big deal in front of the whole group, so they wait. But people rarely talk about what happened after a little time has gone by. They bury the negative feelings associated with the incident and tell each other, "It's not a big deal." Of course, though, those negative feelings don't go away, and they can often transform into long-term dislike.

It's much better to address a short-term conflict quickly, while the emotions are still close to the surface. This is the best time for people to express themselves, listen to another point of view, and legitimately forgive and move on.

Address conflict as a group. Don't feel like you have to act alone in addressing an outbreak of short-term conflict. If something happened within the public view of your group, it can be addressed publicly by the group. Your job as the leader is to highlight what just happened. "I think this conversation is starting to get a little overheated. Does anyone else agree?" Or "I feel like what Henry just said was over the line. What does everyone else think?"

If you're someone like me who really, really doesn't like conflict, saying something like that can seem overwhelming. *How could I call someone out without making them feel attacked? Or shamed?* The answer has less to do with your words and much more to do with your heart. If your group members know you love them and want the best for them, they'll tolerate some honesty. Even correction.

In other words, speak the truth in love.

Use your judgment about moving forward. One of the hardest things to figure out in these kinds of situations is when they're over. When can the group move on and resume the meeting? Since each round of conflict is different, that decision has to be made on a case-by-case basis.

Use your best judgment. If everyone involved seems genuinely sorry for the incident and ready to move forward, then it's over. If one or more people are still smoldering or don't accept the gravity of what just happened, you may need to continue the conversation. And if one or more people are becoming more and more upset, you may need to call a time-out and speak with them privately (or have another trusted group member do so).

If the situation gets to the point where a reasonable solution seems out of the question, you probably need to step in and table the discussion until a later date. Give people a chance to calm down, and then address the issue during the next group meeting at the latest. (If you can get the parties together and figure things out before the next meeting, that's even better.)

When necessary, seek help. As a group leader, don't feel like you have to handle every situation by yourself—especially when there's a clash of personalities or another form of conflict that feels like it could get out of hand. Talk with your church staff. Talk with other trusted members of the group. Seek some wise counsel. And when necessary, seek someone with an elevated level of authority who can step in and enforce any changes that need to be made.

LONG-TERM CONFLICT

Whereas short-term conflict is spontaneous, long-term conflict is more sinister and brooding. Sparked by any number of things— unaddressed short-term conflict, differences in personalities, a perceived insult—long-term conflict can bubble below the surface of relationships indefinitely if left unaddressed.

This kind of conflict carries the potential to seriously damage a community—even cause it to break apart. It puts people walking on eggshells and gradually erodes any feelings of safety and peace initially experienced by the group. For that reason, it needs to be dealt with and resolved in a serious way.

For example, I once had two people in my small group who disliked each other right off the bat. Their personalities clashed, and they were never able to find any common ground. Still, they tried not to make a big deal about it; each person handled the situation by avoiding the other one as much as possible.

After a couple of months, it was clear to me that avoidance was not a long-term solution. When one person made a statement during discussion, the other would automatically disagree. Both individuals started speaking sarcastically to and about the other, and soon the group was inflicted with miniature eruptions of anger and unkind speech. Each group meeting was weighed down by a palpable sense of tension.

Unfortunately, I made the mistake of trying to resolve the issue by serving as a bridge between the two rivals. I had several conversations with each person but always in isolation from the other. I was trying to bring reconciliation by acting like a middle man, and it didn't work. One of the rivals left the group, and the other left a few months later.

So that raises this question: how should a group leader respond in a situation where two or more group members are experiencing serious long-term conflict?

The main job of the group leader in these situations is to talk with each of the people involved and help them see the danger of what's going on and agree to seek a resolution. Then once the rivals are ready to address the problem, you can go about solving it in one of two ways.

First, the rival group members can meet privately with the group leader—and if necessary, with a pastor or mediator as well. This certainly can be effective, and it has certain advantages for keeping private matters private when necessary.

After my failed experience as a middle man, however, I prefer the second option: inviting a pastor or mediator to meet with the whole group and resolving the conflict as a whole-group experience. It's more than likely that everyone in the group is aware of the conflict, and finding a public resolution is effective in bringing healing for the entire group.

To make this happen, I like the conflict-resolution method proposed by Mark Bonham, former executive director of Open Hearts Ministry:[1]

1. The group leader should define the conflict as he/she recalls it. "Our conflict is about the differences between Jim's way and Mary's way of engaging the group and the tension that we and they are experiencing as a result."

2. Ask the group members if the conflict has been defined correctly as they recall it. Go around the circle and give each person an opportunity to respond. Some will have something to say; others may simply nod their head in agreement.
3. Ask, "How has this conflict felt to you?" Or, "What has been stirred up in you as the conflict has become evident?" The purpose here is to give each group member an opportunity to acknowledge and express their feelings. There is no right or wrong answer here. Silence or withholding does not support the conflict resolution process, so encourage everyone to speak.
4. Invite group members to ask questions of any other group member for clarity. Be careful to make sure that one person does not dominate this time so that the process begins to lose momentum for the others.
5. Ask each person, "What were you hoping would happen in this meeting?" "What did you want for yourself?" "What did you want for Jim, Mary, or the group?"
6. Ask each person what needs to happen for them to feel that this is a safe and healthy group again. What a member may express may not necessarily be something the group can guarantee (e.g., that the conflict will never happen again). The leader's role is to make sure all have been heard and to stay engaged in the process for the sake of the group. Allowing the process to stall or wander will make the group feel unsafe and lose trust.
7. Ask each person, "Can you recommit to this group?" If someone says "no," go back to points 3 and 4 and try again. Typically a group will want to get going again and not remain stalled.

Bonham goes on to say, "This process relies on the integrity of the group to call one another out. At its best, it is a way for the body of Christ to minister to each other."[2]

Again, this process should be used only when participants have a major problem affecting the life of the group.

How to Handle Theological Disagreements

No doubt, the Bible is the most influential and important book in human history. It's also incredibly complex.

That's why theological disagreements and debates are so common among Christians. And, yes, theological conflict will pop up regularly in your group. Usually discussions stay pretty tame, and these kinds of discussions are often educational on many levels. But sometimes a theological disagreement can become pretty feisty.

I hate to sound like a broken record, but since every person in every group is different, no canned method of addressing vigorous theological disputes exists. But the following approaches have worked for me and many others. It's up to you as the group leader to choose which method is best for each situation.

TAKE NO ACTION

As I mentioned earlier, most theological debates are harmless—even beneficial. They offer a way for group members to broaden their horizons and be exposed to different points of view. They can serve as an "iron sharpens iron" moment.

So before you take any action to rein in or redirect a theological discussion, ask yourself whether anything harmful is going on. If not, relax and join in the discussion.

USE OUTSIDE AUTHORITY

You may not have seen it, but the chances are very good that the leaders of your church have put together a statement of beliefs or some other document outlining the doctrinal positions the church holds. It's important that you get a copy of this document and keep it handy. Then when a theological debate starts getting a little heated, you can produce it as a source of outside authority: "Here's what our church leaders have written about this particular issue." (Or "Here is the position of our denomination.")

This won't always end the discussion, of course. (Believe it or not, some people out there disagree with their church leaders.) But sometimes it will. And sometimes it will provide a break in the conversation that allows you to suggest an alternate method for resolving the issue, including the methods listed below.

FINISH IT LATER

If your group has engaged in a theological debate that falls within the boundaries of your big idea, that's great. You probably won't want to stop it.

But if group members are going back and forth on an issue that's irrelevant to the main focus of the gathering, as the group leader you're well within your rights to ask them to continue the debate another time. Say something like, "Folks, I know this is an interesting topic, but we should talk about it after we have our final prayer. Let's get back to question 4 in our study guides."

OFFER TO RESEARCH AND RECONVENE

Sometimes a theological conversation goes round and round in circles because it suffers from a lack of information. You'll hear participants say things like, "I'm pretty sure I read that somewhere in the Gospel of John" or "Doesn't Paul say something about salvation and works?" But the discussion doesn't move forward because people can't get a clear view of the theological terrain.

In these situations, you as the group leader should step in and say, "I don't know about everyone else, but I need some more information before I figure out exactly what I believe on this topic. What if we all do some research this week and talk about our discoveries at the next meeting?"

One warning, though: don't use this as a way to get out of a discussion in hopes that your group members lose interest in the topic. Some of them will probably forget doing any research, but not all of them. And those who do work to form an opinion will be disappointed if you ignore their efforts at the next meeting.

ADDRESS HERESY WITH COMPASSION AND TRUTH

There are doctrines of the Christian faith, and then there are essential doctrines—key principles laid out in Scripture that deal directly with our understanding of God, our human condition, and salvation. Denominational differences surrounding what's essential exist, of course, but a large percentage of Christians find agreement over most major historical doctrines.

So what should you do if a group member expresses a belief or opinion that contradicts one of these essential doctrines? Maybe someone casually mentions that they're going to heaven because they're a good person. Maybe someone asserts that the Father, the Son, and the Holy Spirit are different Beings.

Whatever the case, it's important that your first reaction to their statement be one of compassion and kindness. Judgment and condemnation are inappropriate in any situation, including this one. And be sure to avoid giving the impression that they should have known better. It's no good correcting a person's intellectual understanding of Christianity if you violate its core principles in the process.

At the same time, notice I did not say you should react in a way that demonstrates acceptance of false beliefs. Nor should you ignore a clear violation of vital doctrine. As a group leader, you have a responsibility to help your people grow, and this is a prime opportunity.

That being the case, I recommend you take the following steps when confronted with heresy.

> **Label the doctrine under discussion.** To the best of your ability, highlight the theological issue being challenged by the group member's statement or belief. Also give your

impression of the church's position: "I think what we're talking about is the doctrine of the Trinity. The traditional belief is that the Father, the Son, and the Holy Spirit are all the same Being, which is why the Bible talks about 'one God.'"

Invite affirmation from the rest of the group. One thing you don't want to do is get in a one-on-one discussion with the group member in question. Rather, open up the conversation and allow the entire group to be part of it. This should not be an invitation to gang up on a member of your group. The idea is to ask, "What does everyone else think about this issue?" not "Who else wants to explain why this person is wrong?"

Look to sources of authority. All the essential doctrines of Christianity have clear support from the pages of Scripture. So the best opportunity to resolve the issue is for your group to find the passages that relate to the doctrine being discussed. Another option is to seek counsel from your church's statement of beliefs.

Follow up as needed. Helping a group member get a better handle on key doctrinal issues is a great opportunity for growth. So don't miss it. Offer to meet the person for coffee later in the week to discuss the issues in greater detail. Call them a couple of days after the meeting, thank them for their willingness to exchange ideas, and ask if they have any questions now that some time has passed. You can even offer to connect the group member with one of the pastors from the church.

One more thought about addressing theological and doctrinal disagreements in a group: it's worth the effort. It's not always fun, and it can sometimes be a real drag on the momentum of a group meeting—especially when the conversation gets heated or you need to address potential heresy. But it *is* worth it. I feel strongly about this because I feel strongly that doctrine matters. What we believe matters because belief is often the first step toward action and life-change.

Plus, if your group isn't a place for serious discussion about biblical doctrine, where else can your group members turn? Most churchgoers won't walk up to a pastor on Sunday morning and express doubts or confusion about a particular doctrine; nor are they likely to plow through commentaries as if they're light reading.

In today's church, small groups are the best place—and sometimes the only place—for laypeople to clarify what they believe and why they believe it. So don't ignore the opportunity.

When a Bible Study Bombs

No matter how well you choose Bible studies or write your own material, in some group meetings everything will go wrong. The icebreaker is a dud. The discussion questions are more confusing than stimulating. Even the prayer time is uncharacteristically dull.

So how should a group leader react to a clunker of a group meeting?

The best thing to do is honestly share your evaluation with the group. "Folks, I'm feeling like things are a little off tonight. How are the rest of you feeling about the vibe of the group right now?"

If your group members don't share your discomfort, you probably need to just buckle down and continue with the plan. But if your feelings are echoed by the group, you can all work together to come up with a different approach. Maybe people are tired and everyone just needs to relax and have some fun for an hour. Maybe they would like the opportunity to spend more time in prayer or worship or talking about ways to serve.

Whatever you decide, you shouldn't have any trouble declaring a mulligan and getting back into the swing of things the following week.

And that brings up another situation to consider: what if a curriculum is bombing in a more long-term way? Meaning, everyone was excited about a particular Bible study, you all paid for copies of the material, and the group has been using it for a few weeks, but it's not going well. What should you do then?

Again, the best advice is to honestly share your feelings with the group. And if a majority of your group members are dissatisfied with the experience, there's no shame in abandoning a plan. Never be afraid to change what's not working, and never push forward with what's unproductive simply because you don't know what else to do.

When a Group Member Just Doesn't Fit In

If you read much of the content coming out of the small groups world, it won't be long before you come across the subject of group members who don't fit in. The main buzzwords for these individuals are "difficult people" or EGRs (extra grace required).

To be honest, I think a lot of what's been written and produced about this subject is baloney. Or hooey. Or whatever word you prefer to use about a topic people treat as important when it really isn't.

I've said this several times already, but it bears repeating: every group in the world today is made up of human beings. And every human being in the world today is imperfect. We are all sinful. We are all emotional. We are all unpredictable and perplexing and just a bit unstable.

In other words, we're all difficult people. We all require enormous amounts of grace.

That's why I get irritated when I hear things like, "Every group has an EGR person—and if you can't figure out who that person is, it's probably you." Because I don't like the idea of giving a group leader the power to point a finger at a member of the group and say, "He's the difficult one" or "She's the EGR."

No matter our best intentions, labeling an individual that way changes our perception of them. They cease to be an equal member of the group in our eyes—someone to love, serve, and enjoy. Instead, they become someone to manage, someone to control, or someone to avoid.

That's a shame.

I'll get off my soapbox now.

I believe sometimes a truly difficult person does join a small group. And by *difficult* I mean someone with a legitimate psychological or personality disorder.

Some of these individuals have an extreme form of emotional neediness—they dominate entire group meetings by constantly talking about their problems, call people at odd hours, or attempt to reach an uncomfortable level of intimacy with members of the group. This can be a temporary state brought on by a crisis, and even when their struggles are more permanent, these individuals can sometimes function well in a caring and patient group.

Others, however, are incapable of functioning well in social situations. They suffer from conditions like some form of mental illness, a challenging level of autism, or a crippling addiction—something that involves a clinical diagnosis. These individuals may not "work normally" in a typical community.

Here's the problem with these distinctions: if it's a bad idea to label someone as "extra grace required," I certainly don't want to imply that group leaders should start attempting to diagnose clinical disorders. Rather, if a group member is regularly affecting a group in a negative or harmful way, I recommend the following steps.

Get some help. Unless you're a trained counselor, psychologist, or psychiatrist, don't attempt to minister to this kind of person on your own. Consult with a pastor or staff person from your church. Be clear about what you've witnessed from the individual in the group, and don't leave that meeting without a defined plan of action for moving forward.

Set boundaries. If you and your pastor decide the person in question can remain in your group, the next step is to set up a meeting with all three of you. The goal is to establish ground rules and boundaries for the challenged person's participation in the group.

That may sound a little harsh, but it can actually be an encouraging step for the difficult person. Most people who have trouble fitting in with a group are aware of the situation—especially those with emotional issues or social problems. They can sense that something is wrong, that people are uncomfortable around them, but they usually can't put a finger on the specific causes. So having a meeting to establish boundaries gives these individuals something to focus on and a goal for improvement.

Inform the group. You can inform the group by holding a group meeting without the difficult person or by meeting with or calling group members one at a time. One purpose of these meetings is to bring group members up to speed on both the difficulty faced by the person in question and the boundaries set in place to help them become integrated into group life. A second purpose is to rally the group around the potential for genuinely life-changing ministry this individual represents. They have the chance to represent Christ in a powerful way.

Adopt the last resort. Including a truly difficult person in a small group will be hard. And although the rewards can be substantial—both for the person in question and the other group members—sometimes their inclusion simply doesn't work out. If you as the group leader feel the situation is becoming unbearable for the group, you should again meet with your pastor and talk about removing the person from the group. This should be the last option explored, but it does need to be an option.

If you ask the individual to leave the group, work with your pastor to present them with another option for community involvement. This could include a support group or regular sessions with a pastor or counselor.

Chapter 14

Application and Inspiration

It was my first voluntary memory verse. Sure, I had memorized John 3:16 and other famous Scripture verses as part of my Sunday school attendance, but as I set out to read through the book of James on New Year's Eve in what was then my junior year of high school, I got stuck near the end of the very first chapter: "Do not merely listen to the word, and so deceive yourselves. Do what it says" (James 1:22).

Reading that verse felt like a hammer blow to my spirit. It stopped me in my tracks. Maybe for the first time in my life, I felt like the Bible was talking directly to me.

See, at that point in my spiritual journey, I had done a lot of listening to the Word. Sermons. Sunday school teachers. Books. I took pride in knowing the right thing to say to impress the authority figures around me. (I also took pride in my reputation as a Bible trivia master.) But in the back of my mind, I was aware that my heart wasn't fully connected to my mind. I knew a lot of stuff, but I didn't do a lot of stuff.

Then came James 1:22. To this day, that verse still sends shivers up my spine. And it remains a reminder for me to never settle for knowing information at the expense of spiritual transformation—at the expense of doing what the Scripture says.

Not just me, though. James 1:22 is a command, which means it applies to all followers of Jesus, including your group members. And including your group as a whole. That's why we need to make application part of our group gatherings.

Tips and Tricks

Like most aspects of group ministry, there's no "right" way to do application. You can use lots of methods to obey God's Word personally and to provide opportunities for your group to do the same.

Sometimes, though, it's still good to have outside suggestions. So here are a few tips and tricks that can help you make obedience a high priority for your group.

GET IT ON THE CALENDAR

As a group leader, one of the best things you can do when it comes to application is to proactively lead your group members into situations that allow them to obey what they've learned. They can be service projects, mission trips, prayer walks, evangelistic opportunities, or anything else you can think of. Get some events on everyone's calendar, and make it clear that application is an "official" part of your group.

You don't have to take the lead on this yourself. If another person in the group shows an affinity for doing something tangible to obey God's commands, consider making them the Application Champion for the group (or whatever title works best). Empower that person to regularly present opportunities for obedience before the group and to assist you in the administration of those opportunities.

DESEGREGATE APPLICATION IN YOUR GROUP MEETINGS

Too many group studies and curriculum options contain an "application section" at the end of each session's material. This is usually a one-sentence piece of encouragement based on the topic covered during the discussion—"Look for ways to love your neighbors as you go about your life this week."

Bah! Why separate application from the rest of your group's time together?

As an alternative, keep a sharp eye out for biblical commands and outward-facing principles during every part of your gathering. One example would be direct commands contained in Scripture—like James 1:22, for example. Other examples are inferred commands in the Bible, group members expressing a desire to "do something," and prayer requests that provide an opportunity for direct action.

When you see one of those opportunities, highlight it for your group and start a conversation about practical obedience right then and there. For example, say, "All right, it's pretty clear that Jesus is commanding us to visit people in prison. How can we make that happen as a group in the next couple of weeks?"

BRING ACCOUNTABILITY INTO THE CONVERSATION

What if you asked an accountability question each time your group got together? Like, "Last week we talked about the importance of regularly submitting to God's Word. So how many of us read the Bible at least five times this week?" The goal of a question like that is not to embarrass anyone or be judgmental. Rather, it sends the message that obedience is the expected reaction to God's commands.

USE POSITIVE REINFORCEMENT

One of the best ways to prevent application and accountability from becoming judgmental is to regularly celebrate the times group members do obey and apply God's Word. This can range from a simple acknowledgment—"I'm really proud of you, Jennifer"—to a literal party where you highlight the progress made by everyone in the group.

You can make application an important part of your group experience in lots of ways. The point is to make the effort to not just hear but obey.

Inward and Outward

Right about now you might be thinking, *I have the ability to apply Scripture and obey God on my own just as part of my regular spiritual life. So why do I need to make application part of my group? Isn't each member capable of doing that as well?*

The answer has to do with your group's focus when it comes to your community. Namely, a lack of application can cause the group to have only an inward focus, which is harmful. Let's dig a little deeper to see what I mean.

Outwardly focused groups seek to engage the world. They're aware of what's happening in their congregation and in the broader community that surrounds them. They make it a priority to serve people in need, sometimes to the point of keeping in touch with international missionaries and the like.

Inwardly focused groups are just the opposite. They view their group as a way to huddle against the world—although they think of it in terms of building existing relationships within the group. This sounds good in theory, but more often than not, the group ends up breaking apart due to interpersonal conflict.

In other words, outwardly focused groups are vibrant, healthy, and growing. Inwardly focused groups are protective, territorial, and dying.

And unfortunately, there usually isn't a lot of middle ground between the two. I think of what Big Tom Callahan says in the movie *Tommy Boy*: "When it comes to auto parts, son, you're either growin' or you're dyin'. There ain't no third direction." The same is true when it comes to most facets of spiritual growth and transformation, including in small groups.

Right about now you might be thinking, *I'm going to make sure my small group has an outward focus.* And I hope it does. But groups rarely become outwardly or inwardly focused as a result of some arbitrary choice. Nobody would consciously choose to set up a selfish, dying group, would they?

No, the path to becoming inwardly or outwardly focused is more complicated than a single choice, and it's always centered on obedience. After all, any productive group will be regularly exposed to the commands of God through the Bible, the Holy Spirit, and the witness of other Christians. Those commands include "Love your neighbor as yourself," "Make disciples of all nations," "Give generously," and "Look after orphans and widows in their distress."

Groups that consistently live out these commands (and the others like it) become outwardly focused. Groups that consistently ignore these commands become inwardly focused. It really is that simple.

And that's why application is critical not just for you but for your group.

Final Word

As we arrive at the final page of this journey together, I hope you feel both equipped and inspired to engage the critical work of leading your group. Remember, you're part of a noble tradition that stretches back thousands of years, and you have a direct role to play in the spiritual lives and spiritual growth of those entrusted to your care.

This is amazing news! This is an incredible opportunity! And yes, leading a group is an important responsibility.

Thankfully, the rewards are amazing.

One final word of advice: you're going to make mistakes. Things will happen in the group you'll later wish had not happened. Somebody may feel offended. Somebody may feel excluded. You may botch a study or miss a chance to invite someone new or crash and burn while trying to lead an activity that seemed like a slam dunk during your preparation time.

You will make mistakes as a group leader. Probably lots of mistakes. And that's okay.

Really, that's wonderful. Because making mistakes is how we grow. Making mistakes is often the best way to learn something new—not just learn the information but really assimilate the principle. And most mistakes are correctable.

If someone feels offended during a gathering, you can talk with them afterward and apologize. If someone is excluded or you miss a chance to invite someone new, you can take whatever steps necessary to create another opportunity. And if you crash and burn with a learning activity, you can join with everyone else in laughing at your miss—and then you can move on.

So take what you've learned in these pages and jump with both feet into the work and privilege of leading your group. Be bold. Make mistakes. Serve God.

And be blessed!

Notes

INTRODUCTION

1. Ben Renner, "Survey: Quarter of Americans Feel They Have No One to Confide In," Study Finds, May 27, 2019, https://www.studyfinds.org /survey-quarter-americans-have-no-one-confide/.

CHAPTER 1: SMALL GROUPS 101

1. Eugene Peterson, *Eat This Book* (Grand Rapids: Eerdmans, 2006).

CHAPTER 2: THE MINISTRY OF DISCIPLESHIP

1. Statista Research Department, "How often do you attend church or synagogue at least once a week, almost every week, about once a month, seldom, or never?," Statista.com, January 24, 2022, https://www.statista.com/statistics/245491/church-attendance -of-americans/.

CHAPTER 3: THE MINISTRY OF HOSPITALITY

1. Will Miller and Glenn Sparks, *Refrigerator Rights* (New York: Penguin Putnam, 2002).
2. Will Miller, "What Are Refrigerator Rights?," *Refrigerator Rights*, November 2, 2006, www.fridgerights.blogspot.com.
3. Stephanie Voiland Rische, "The Theology of Huckleberry Pie," *Today's Christian Woman* (from the SmallGroups.com training resource "Hospitality in Your Small Group"), September 2007,

https://www.todaychristianwoman.com/articles/2007/september/theology-of-huckleberry-pie.html.

4. Jim Egli, "A Small Group Leader's Most Important Job," SmallGroups.com, February 15, 2010, https://www.smallgroups.com/articles/2010/small-group-leaders-most-important-job.html.

5. Egli, "A Small Group Leader's Most Important Job."

6. Egli, "A Small Group Leader's Most Important Job."

7. Egli, "A Small Group Leader's Most Important Job."

8. Egli, "A Small Group Leader's Most Important Job."

9. Randall Neighbour, "How to Host a Small Group Meeting," SmallGroups.com, March 12, 2008, https://www.smallgroups.com/articles/2008/how-to-host-small-group-meeting.html.

CHAPTER 4: ARE SMALL GROUPS STILL RELEVANT?

1. Christopher Smith, "Drive In Church Services Turn Parking Lots into Pews," Motor1, March 30, 2020, https://www.motor1.com/news/406967/drive-in-church-services/.

2. Diana Bennett, "A Brief History of Small Groups (part 2)," SmallGroups.com, accessed March 23, 2022, https://www.smallgroups.com/articles/2011/brief-history-of-small-groups-part-2.html.

3. Elena Renken, "Most Americans Are Lonely, and Our Workplace Culture May Not Be Helping," NPR, January 23, 2020, https://www.npr.org/sections/health-shots/2020/01/23/798676465/most-americans-are-lonely-and-our-workplace-culture-may-not-be-helping.

4. Ceylan Yeginsu, "U.K. Appoints a Minister for Loneliness," *New York Times*, January 17, 2018, https://www.nytimes.com/2018/01/17/world/europe/uk-britain-loneliness.html.

5. Jeffrey M. Jones, "U.S. Church Membership Falls Below Majority for First Time," Gallup, March 29, 2021, https://news.gallup.com/poll/341963/church-membership-falls-below-majority-first-time.aspx.

6. Mary Jahnke, "Millennials & Gen Z Are Leaving Church. What Can We Do?," Faithlife, May 27, 2021, https://blog.faithlife.com/millennials-gen-z-leaving-church/.

7. Jahnke, "Millennials & Gen Z Are Leaving Church. What Can We Do?"

CHAPTER 5: LEARNING STYLES

1. David Kolb's ELT model of learning styles is probably the best-known system. See his book *Experiential Learning: Experience as the Source of Learning and Development* (Upper Saddle River, NJ: Prentice Hall, 1984). Other models are explained and evaluated in Robert Sternberg's book *Thinking Styles* (New York: Cambridge University Press, 1999).
2. For more information on the VARK model, see Neil Fleming, *Teaching and Learning Styles: VARK Strategies* (Neil Fleming, 2006) and "VARK: A Guide to Learning Styles," 2010, www.vark-learn.com.
3. Names for any people referenced in my current or former small groups have been changed.
4. Fleming, *Teaching and Learning Styles.*

CHAPTER 8: CRAFTING GREAT DISCUSSION QUESTIONS

1. I first heard the phrase *idiot question* from Larry Osborne in the "Small Groups Starter Kit" produced by North Coast Church in 2008.

CHAPTER 12: LEADING WELL-ROUNDED GROUP MEETINGS

1. Andrew Wheeler, *Together in Prayer* (Downers Grove, IL: InterVarsity, 2009), 39.
2. Wheeler, *Together in Prayer,* 40.

CHAPTER 13: WHEN A GROUP MEETING DOESN'T GO AS PLANNED

1. Mark Bonham, "Engaging Conflict in Small Groups," SmallGroups. com, August 6, 2008, www.smallgroups.com/articles/2008 /engagingconflictinsmallgroups.html.
2. Bonham, "Engaging Conflict in Small Groups."